Racialized Coverage
of Congress

Racialized Coverage —— of Congress ——

The News in Black and White

Jeremy Zilber and David Niven

PRAEGER

Westport, Connecticut
London

Library of Congress Cataloging-in-Publication Data

Zilber, Jeremy, 1966–
    Racialized coverage of Congress : the news in Black and white / Jeremy Zilber and
David Niven.
        p.   cm.
    Includes bibliographical references and index.
    ISBN 0–275–96841–3 (alk. paper)
    1. Afro-American legislators.   2. United States—Race relations—Political aspects. 3.
Afro-Americans in mass media.   4. United States. Congress—Press coverage.
5. Press and politics—United States.   I. Niven, David, 1971–   II. Title.
E185.615.N58   2000
328.73'008996073—dc21   99–059656

British Library Cataloguing in Publication Data is available.

Library of Congress Catalog Card Number: 99–059656
ISBN: 0–275–96841–3

First published in 2000

Praeger Publishers, 88 Post Road West, Westport, CT 06881
An imprint of Greenwood Publishing Group, Inc.
www.praeger.com

Printed in the United States of America

The paper used in this book complies with the
Permanent Paper Standard issued by the National
Information Standards Organization (Z39.48–1984).

10 9 8 7 6 5 4 3 2 1

To my parents — JZ

To Barbara Brown — DN

To fail to understand is the surest guarantee of a mounting strife which will assault the well-being of every citizen. . . . For the division between black and white is not the result of a failure of compassion, or of the American sense of justice. It is a failure of communication and vision.

—Robert F. Kennedy, speaking at Michigan State University, April 11, 1968

Contents

Tables

Acknowledgments

We appreciate the generosity of the congressional press secretaries and congressional reporters who took the time to share their thoughts with us. Without their participation, this study could not have been done.

Our efforts have also benefited considerably from the able research assistance of Jason Bumiller, Karen Greer, Christine Lefkowitz, Erica Patterson, Michael Strong, and Brian Tierney.

We thank Rosalee Clawson and Sarah Pines for their helpful comments and suggestions on this project.

Our research was supported by grants from the American Political Science Association and the Florida Atlantic University Research Initiation Fund. A previous version of Chapter 3 appeared in the *Harvard International Journal of Press/Politics*.

Finally, we gratefully acknowledge the support and encouragement of our colleagues in the Department of Government at the College of William and Mary and the Department of Political Science at Florida Atlantic University and the contributions, both direct and indirect, of our graduate school professors in the Department of Political Science at Ohio State University.

1

Introduction: Race, Media, and Politics

Perhaps nowhere have African Americans gained more political ground since the passage of the 1965 Voting Rights Act than in the House of Representatives. Numbering a mere 6 in 1966, the 106th Congress can now boast 37 African American members,[1] many of whom have risen to positions of institutional and national prominence. Yet, it would be laughable to assume that increased representation in the House has translated into political equality. Virtually all of the African American members were elected in districts where white voters are in the minority, suggesting that our electoral system is far from color-blind and far from equal. For additional evidence of continuing racial disparity one need look no further than the more prestigious house of Congress, the Senate, where African Americans are completely absent. At the state level, no African American currently occupies either a governor's seat or state attorney general's office.

Equally troubling is the degree to which race and racial issues remain such deeply divisive factors in American politics. When asked for their opinions on African Americans, whites are surprisingly willing to reveal a significant number of stereotypical beliefs. A prominent 1992 survey found that a majority (57%) of white Americans believe African Americans are lazier than whites, and nearly half (49%) claimed that African Americans are less intelligent (Entman 1997). Moreover, African

Americans' perception of whites is also negative, with large numbers perceiving that whites hold racist opinions (Sigelman and Tuch 1997).

Indeed, survey research consistently demonstrates that whites and African Americans share few of the same beliefs, attitudes, or priorities, leading one group of public opinion scholars to write that "no other demographic groups in America have more different opinions than blacks and whites" (Glynn, Herbst, O'Keefe, and Shapiro 1999, 232). On the whole, African Americans are much more likely to see themselves as treated unfairly by public officials and the police, to support government-sponsored programs to eradicate inequalities, and to view racism as a significant social problem. Conversely, the majority of white Americans seem relatively satisfied with the current treatment of African Americans, and an overwhelming majority oppose affirmative action programs offering preferential treatment in schools and the workplace (Glynn, Herbst, O'Keefe, and Shapiro 1999).

Calling racial differences "a divide without peer," Donald Kinder and Lynn Sanders reach the same conclusion in their 1996 book, *Divided by Color*. But they also add that differences between whites and African Americans are common occurrences in matters having nothing to do with race:

To be sure, the radical divide is most pronounced over policies that bear unambiguously and differentially on the fortunes of black and white. But the divide is also apparent on issues where the racial implications are unstated and covert, on the desirability of the American version of the welfare state and on distrust of government. Such differences recall the Kerner Commission's warnings of a quarter-century ago, issued in the midst of the urban riots of the 1960s, that the United States was drifting towards two societies, one white, the other black. On many matters of public policy, black and white Americans do seem to live in different worlds. (31)

While many Americans (including some elected officials) seem prepared to accept this state of affairs as "natural," and perhaps it would be naive to expect that racial differences will ever entirely vanish, the underlying premise of this book is that the existence of dramatic racial disparities — in terms of both holding opinions and holding public office — is anything *but* a natural state of affairs. Our efforts are guided by the overarching principle that individuals' opinions and political prospects ought not to be easily inferred from their skin color. We should be striving for a politics where, in the words of novelist Toni Morrison, "race exits, but does not matter." Far from accepting the current situation as either normal or expected, we are forced to conclude that something has gone terribly wrong in American politics.

As the book's title suggests and as will soon become evident, we contend that the American news media have contributed significantly to the problem. This is not at all to say that we hold the media responsible for historical racial inequality nor that the media are the sole reason for its perseverance. Obviously, the question of racial equality is ultimately in the hands of the American public, which is, after all, the final arbiter of what it thinks and whom it elects. However, we are steadfastly convinced that many standard media practices — particularly those relating to covering African American public officials — are contributing to a state of perpetual racial disharmony in American politics.

MEDIA POWER IN POLIITCS

While many media scholars have spent the last few decades debating the precise boundaries of media influence, few would dispute the assertion that news coverage plays a significant role in shaping public opinion. According to noted media expert Doris Graber, it would be hard to overstate the press' public sway:

How journalists cover stories often plays a crucial part in shaping the perceptions of reality of millions of people in all walks of life. . . . Media stories . . . indicate what is deemed important or unimportant by various groups of elites, what conforms to prevailing standards of justice and morality, and how events are related to each other. In the process the media present a set of cultural values that their audience are likely to accept in whole or in part as typical of American society. (1997, 3)

Reporters are obviously not omnipotent manipulators of public opinion, but they are often asked to serve as citizens' primary (if not only) link to political actors and events. This is especially true for national politics, where the most significant events usually take place overseas or in distant Washington, D.C. Simply put, what we know about politics often depends a great deal on what we are told by the media. Having few independent sources of information on national affairs, most citizens find themselves at the mercy of news coverage in formulating their political opinions.

Moreover, the media's influence in American politics has almost certainly been on the rise throughout the past two decades. Cable television now offers the average American a variety of programming options from which to choose, including round-the-clock coverage from stations devoted exclusively to news. With the rise of several new communication technologies, most notably the Internet, the reach of mass media has been increased further still.

Concurrent with the onslaught of new media outlets has been an equally important decline in traditional socializing forces. Political parties, once dominant in most voters' decision-making equations, have for a number of reasons seen their influence steadily decay since their heyday in the 1930s and 1940s. Parents, too, have begun to play a reduced role in shaping children's political opinions and activities (Jennings and Niemi 1981; Kahan 1999). In the absence of strong guidance from these two traditional agents of socialization, Americans — especially young Americans — are arguably more susceptible to media images today than at any time in our history (Kahan 1999).

Influential media are not in and of themselves a problem, but they become a problem when the information presented is deceptive or fails to accurately reflect reality. While we cherish our First Amendment right to a free press, we must be equally vigilant in guarding against its abuse. Errors of fact or judgment are bound to happen from time to time, but a systematic pattern of deception or misrepresentation is potentially quite harmful. Almost by definition a democracy requires a well-informed citizenry, and our citizenry can hope to be only as informed as the information it receives.

Several recent opinion polls have shown that a majority of Americans disapprove of the way their news is presented and distrust the mass media as an institution.[2] One might therefore be tempted to assume that most Americans are selective consumers of news, constantly on guard for potentially false or misleading information. In reality, though, it would be hard for even the most skeptical among us to spot anything but the most blatant cases of reporter bias. Common sense dictates that the average American sitting at home watching the nightly news or reading the local newspaper will have a difficult time discerning whether any given story is slanted, poorly researched, or unrepresentative.[3]

Moreover, news consumers could hardly be considered a captive audience. With so many news outlets from which to choose, we naturally tend to gravitate toward the sources we believe most trustworthy. Thus, while Americans may distrust the media as an *institution*, they are apt to assume that most of the news they personally receive will be a fairly accurate representation of reality — all the more reason to believe that a systematic pattern of faulty news reporting is likely to produce erroneous public judgments on a variety of topics.

MEDIA "BIAS"

That there may be a systematic slant in news coverage would hardly be an original claim. Politicians from both ends of the ideological spectrum have long been accusing the media of a political agenda favoring their opponents. Allegations of a "liberal bias" are most common, but many on the left have argued that mainstream media reflect the views of the wealthy and powerful, while favoring the status quo.

Most reputable academic studies have concluded that the truth lies somewhere in between. While it is widely agreed that reporters are, on average, more liberal than the general public, we also know that reporters usually attempt to remain objective when reporting on politics (Beyle, Ostdiek, and Lynch 1996). Like most professionals, journalists are expected to check their personal biases and opinions at the door when they come to work.   Beyond an expectation of objectivity, the journalistic process involves more than just the reporter; editors and owners (who tend to be more conservative than reporters), support staff, and even advertisers all play some role in shaping the final news product. Rarely are reporters allowed to decide the headline or placement of their stories, for example. Thus, as Gans (1980) has argued, the larger process of selecting, writing, and editing stories usually weeds out whatever traces of partisan bias might otherwise have appeared in a reporter's work.

Researchers have shown, for example, that news coverage of presidential campaigns has been mostly neutral, reflecting no apparent favoritism toward one party or the other (Hofstetter 1976; Graber 1997; Robinson and Sheehan 1983; Just 1997). Studies focusing on particular issues have reached similar conclusions; that is, controversial issues tend to be presented in neutral terms (Bennett 1990; Dickson 1994; Zaller and Chiu 1996). Thus, despite many allegations and counter allegations from liberal and conservative Democrats and Republicans, most of the news we receive does not seem to have a consistent partisan bias one way or the other (Niven 1999).

But to say that media reporting is generally free from partisan bias is not to say that it accurately represents the people and events being covered. Indeed, bias is an elusive concept, meaning different things to different people, and only in a very narrow sense of the term — preferential partisan treatment — would it be accurate to say the media have assumed an unbiased posture.

In their book *By Invitation Only*, David Croteau and William Hoynes explore the problem of using the term "bias" as a synonym for "favoritism," noting that *what* the media choose to report (or not report) is just as problematic as *how* they choose to report it. Where traditional charges of media bias imply either an inaccuracy on the journalist's part (whether intended or not) or a failure to tell "both sides" of the story, bias also exists if journalists consistently choose to focus disproportionate attention on certain kinds of stories or put undue emphasis on certain aspects of events while ignoring or underplaying others. As summarized by Croteau and Hoynes:

News media coverage, in fact, does not reflect some objective reality "out there" in the "real" world. Instead, news is the result of a social process through which media personnel make decisions about what is newsworthy and what is not, about who is important and who is not, about what views are to be included in debates and what views can be dismissed. None of these decisions can be totally objective ones. Instead, rarely articulated assumptions underlie the approach news media take in making such decisions. (1994, 31)

Interestingly, Croteau and Hoynes' argument closely mirrors an admonition offered to journalists in the *New York Times Manual of Style and Usage*:

Fairness and accuracy should be the hallmark of all news articles. . . . Obviously, accuracy is a chief element of fairness and impartiality. But accuracy is easily subverted. For instance, a number of facts, each accurate, can be juxtaposed and presented in a tendentious, unfair manner. Even simple, seemingly innocent words can be employed with the same resulting partiality. And even background information can be manipulated (most easily by its mere use or omission) to the detriment of fairness. (1976, 75)

These two passages make several very important points and collectively lay a foundation for the central argument of this book. The writers present a paradigm in which news may be entirely accurate and ideologically neutral yet still biased in that it systematically focuses on a narrow range of issues, people, events, or ideas.

Imagine, for example, a congressional reporter who covers only the bills expected to pass by nearly unanimous votes. There would be no misrepresentation of the facts; each bill and each vote would be reported accurately. Likewise, there can be no claims of ideological favoritism, because each piece of legislation would obviously enjoy widespread support among both parties. Yet, it would clearly be fair to label this type of reporting "biased" because it systematically over reports a special type of event while ignoring more typical events.[4] Widespread reporting of this nature would obviously leave the public with a distorted sense of the legislative process, as most citizens would probably infer that most congressional decisions are relatively consensual.[5]

Moreover, unlike traditional charges of bias that erroneously assume that reporters' personal opinions will be allowed to dictate the substance and tone of the news, our paradigm describes a type of bias that is not specific to the reporter who happens to be writing the story. Rather, it describes a journalistic disposition shaped more by a "social process" and "rarely articulated assumptions" than the individual reporter's preexisting beliefs and opinions.

In other words, we can easily imagine a few biases that may be virtually universal within the media industry, biases that are pervasive among not just reporters but editorial and administrative staff as well. By definition, such industry-wide bias would color the work of both liberal and conservative members of the media, leaving no one to act as a neutral referee to call "fouls." Such a ubiquitous bias could go virtually unnoticed, but its effects on public opinion would be potentially limitless.

Indeed, a number of potentially damaging media biases have been brought to light in recent years. Both print and broadcast news have been accused of giving too much attention to scandal, controversy, celebrities, crime, tragedy, and other "human interest" topics, while eschewing many of the mundane, complex, and abstract issues that have more impact on Americans' lives. Academics have been at the forefront of these critiques (see, e.g., Bennett 1988; Patterson 1994; Graber 1997), but similar charges have been leveled by independent watchdog organizations such as Fairness and Accuracy in Reporting (FAIR), and many of the same complaints are frequently raised in Internet news group discussions devoted to current events and media coverage.

Some of these criticisms have even been echoed by members of the mainstream media themselves. CNN, for example, features a weekly roundtable discussion (*Reliable Sources*) in which noted journalists catalog instances of sloppy or sensationalized media coverage. Similar concerns are also recurrent themes on radio talk shows, as well as network programs such as *Nightline* and *This Week*. Some of the most scathing commentary comes from the former editor of *U.S. News and World Report*, James Fallows, whose book *Breaking the News: How the Media Undermine American Democracy* denounces the mass media for allowing the profit motive to dictate both the substance and style of news presentations. Many of the same accusations can be found in *Brill's Content*, the first mainstream magazine devoted entirely to evaluating and critiquing the mass media's performance.

While these are legitimate criticisms with which we wholeheartedly agree, they have been widely recognized and well documented for some time now. Although we find little to suggest that mainstream media have taken significant steps toward appeasing their critics, we take mild comfort in knowing that news professionals are well aware of the criticisms. Unfortunately, short of removing the words "freedom of the press" from the First Amendment, little can be done to correct the problem other than remaining vigilant in pointing out instances of journalistic misbehavior. Hopefully, industry leaders will eventually take it upon themselves to institute serious reform.

RACIALIZED REPORTING

Scholars and watchdog organizations are absolutely correct to point out instances of shoddy or sensational journalism. Unfortunately, comparatively little attention has been given to the effect that reporting on minority politicians may have on the way Americans think about race and gender relations, minority issues, or minorities themselves. The dearth of commentary is especially alarming in light of the widespread racial disharmony discussed earlier and even more surprising given what is known about the causal links between images on the news and the public's behavior. This relationship is described in some detail in Chapter 5, but for now suffice it to say that we expect to find a direct connection between the substance and style of news presentations and what the public thinks and does. We believe, for example, that coverage of minorities is likely to influence the way the public thinks about a group as a whole.

Thus, if we are serious about tackling the problem of race relations, we need to start paying more attention to the way minorities are portrayed in the news.

What scant research does exist all seems to point in the same general direction: news coverage of African Americans is inadequate, frequently inaccurate, and arguably more harmful than helpful. Studies examining coverage in the 1960s, 1970s, and 1980s are critical of the media for failing to adequately cover African Americans and other minorities.[6] In her examination of four major newspapers during the 1960s and 1970s, Carolyn Martindale (1986) found that media coverage of African Americans had improved over time but continued to pay relatively little attention to African Americans' day-to-day problems and disproportionately portrayed them as criminals, athletes, and entertainers.

A more recent study argues that news programs on the major network affiliates in Chicago are disproportionately likely to feature whites as law enforcers, helpers, or Good Samaritans, while minorities are more likely to be portrayed as criminals (Entman 1997). A similar study by Martin Gilens (1995) concludes that national newsmagazines from 1988 to 1992 were far more likely to picture African Americans than whites in stories relating to poverty, despite the fact that the overwhelming majority of poor Americans are white. Gilens also finds that the most sympathetic groups of impoverished African Americans, the elderly and working poor, are underrepresented relative to their absolute numbers and comparable white groups. "Not only do African Americans as a whole suffer from the exaggerated association of race and poverty, but poor African Americans (who are often the intended beneficiaries of race-targeted policies) are portrayed in a particularly negative light" (25).

African American political figures have not fared much better. In a 1980 study of newspaper coverage of white and African American elected officials in cities with large minority populations, Anju Chaudhary discovered that white candidates were more likely to receive prominent story placement (front page or above the fold) and were also more likely to be portrayed in a positive light. Stories on African American politicians were, on average, slightly longer than those on whites, but whites nevertheless received significantly more overall coverage on Election Day. Generally speaking, when African Americans run for office, the media tend to emphasize their race, while typically ignoring the race or ethnicity of white candidates. Coverage of elections with at least one

African American candidate is also likely to emphasize racial issues such as affirmative action (Terkildsen 1996).

Croteau and Hoynes (1994) examined the characteristics of guests appearing on two widely acclaimed news programs, ABC's *Nightline* and PBS's *MacNeil/Lehrer NewsHour*, over a six-month span in 1989. Not surprisingly, African Americans and other minorities were significantly underrepresented (non whites accounted for approximately 11% of the guests on both programs) and virtually nonexistent for topics not directly related to "minority issues." On the topic of the economy, for example, 50 of the 52 invited guests were white, as were all 32 who appeared on segments devoted to the environment.

Robert Entman's investigation of news coverage of African American political leaders paints an even darker portrait:

Direct quotes (sound bites) from black activists, politicians or officials made them appear much more selfish and demanding than their white counterparts. In one study, some 33 percent of all assertions made by blacks endorsing or criticizing a government policy demanded attention to the black community. Whites explicitly promoted their ethnic group interests only 5 percent of the time. Indeed, white leaders were shown more often explicitly defending black political interests than openly advancing their own group's self interests. (1997, 31)

Entman also points to the remarkable proportion of stories on African American leaders accused of wrongdoing. He notes that in one year of national network news coverage, over a third of the stories mentioning an African American leader involved some sort of criminal accusation. Naturally, given white leaders' greater prominence in national politics, the percentage of stories mentioning whites' involvement in criminal behavior is typically much smaller. In the year Entman conducted his research, for instance, the two most frequently mentioned African American political figures were Supreme Court justice Clarence Thomas, who was accused of sexual harassment, and Washington, D.C., mayor Marion Barry, who was arrested and convicted for possession of cocaine. As Entman puts it:

The coverage of Barry's drug arrest accurately reflected the experience of a scurrilous politician who happened to be black. But there are hundreds of effective, conscientious black mayors toiling around the Unites States who together attained only a fraction of the network visibility accorded Barry. . . . Nonetheless, given how prejudiced people process information, we can predict that the accurate but frequent and sensational reports of Barry's crimes, arrest and conviction promoted inaccurate stereotypes among many whites. (1997, 32)

There is a near consensus among African American political leaders that they are being unfairly portrayed. A 1988 study of African American state legislators revealed virtually universal agreement that stories on crime were unfair to African Americans. Legislators also complained of inadequate coverage in minority communities, and 89% thought that more African American reporters should be hired in order to improve coverage (Sneed, Riffe, and Van Ommeren 1988).

A number of the nation's most prominent African American politicians, such as former Los Angeles mayor and California gubernatorial candidate Tom Bradley, former New York mayor David Dinkins, former representative and Chicago mayor Harold Washington, and former presidential candidate Jesse Jackson, have experienced this kind of separate and unequal coverage during their careers (Pettigrew and Alston 1988; Payne 1988; Reeves 1997; Grainey, Pollack, and Kusmierek 1984; Kleppner 1985; Gibbons 1993). Nationwide, most African American elected officials at all levels of government believe that media coverage is unequal and tilted against them (Riffe, Sneed, and Van Ommeren 1989).

While academic research supporting these claims is relatively thin, several studies on media coverage of women in politics have reached similar conclusions. Content analyses have demonstrated that female Senate candidates, including incumbent senators, are more likely to be portrayed as politically vulnerable. Also, more attention is paid to "female issues," such as child care, when reporters are covering women's campaigns (Kahn 1996). Women politicians are also less likely to be cited or quoted in news articles or selected as guests on network news programs (Weaver and Wilhoit 1996; Clawson and Tom 1999; Croteau and Hoynes 1994).

While there has not yet been a definitive study of minority media coverage, a clear picture begins to unfold. For reasons discussed at length in the chapters to follow, many reporters appear to be drawn to minority politicians' "otherness," perhaps even to the point of ignoring issues that really matter to the politicians themselves. Consider, for example, the following excerpt from a Knight-Ridder story on John Conyers (D-MI), the ranking Democrat on the House Judiciary Committee, which ran during the Clinton impeachment hearings:

A generation after the Watergate scandal that brought down Richard Nixon, Michigan's John Conyers . . . has become a pivotal player as Congress once again considers impeaching a president. The bespectacled, 17-term Congressman from Detroit with the even-toned voice and brushed-back hair has been everywhere: On NBC verbally trouncing anti-Clinton author Bill Bennett; on CSPAN pleading for a delayed release of the independent counsel's report on Clinton's affair with Monica Lewinsky; on the House floor making the same arguments. Colleagues describe Conyers, who grew up in Detroit, as a mannerly gentleman who might greet a fellow lawyer as "counselor." When Detroit gained a majority-black district in 1964, he ran for it and won, becoming the second black person to represent the city in Congress. He became the consummate grassroots advocate, thriving on the turbulence of Vietnam and the Civil Rights era. He went to sit-ins. Fifteen years ago, Conyers successfully pushed through a bill to create a Martin Luther King holiday. Five years ago, he gave a memorable tongue-lashing to U.S. Attorney-General Janet Reno after the botched FBI raid on the Branch Davidian compound in Waco, Texas.[7]

This seemingly innocuous portrait is precisely the sort of reporting that we find so troubling. In an article ostensibly inspired by his prominent role in the impeachment process, Representative Conyers has been reduced to little more than a black man from a black district whose entire political career revolves around civil rights. Completely lost in this description are Conyers' 34 years of legislative accomplishments in areas such as foreign policy, health care, crime and drugs, jobs creation, and government waste — the very issues Conyers himself identifies as his most pressing concerns.[8]

Of course, a single article about a single member of Congress will have no measurable effect on public opinion, but consider the potential impact that hundreds and hundreds of similar stories might have on a population relying almost exclusively on mass media for its political news. In the absence of disconfirming information, even the most attentive of Conyers' constituents might reasonably infer their congressman is largely preoccupied with racial matters and, by default, largely *un*interested in more general political issues.

SCOPE AND EFFECTS OF RACIALIZED REPORTING OF CONGRESS

Both anecdotal evidence and prior research suggest that African American politicians receive distinct media coverage, but the extent of the problem is not well known. Most of the studies cited earlier focused on candidates for political office, and virtually all focused on state or local offices. This leaves several questions yet to be carefully explored:

1. *To what extent is racialized media coverage the norm for sitting members of Congress?* The media have often been accused of focusing on racial conflict in political campaigns (perhaps even injecting it themselves), but what happens when minority *candidates* become minority *officeholders*? Existing evidence appears to suggest that racialized coverage does not stop on election day, but the evidence is still too scant to draw firm conclusions. Moreover, it seems plausible that racialized coverage might lessen as we move up the political ladder. As members of the world's most powerful legislative body, perhaps minority members of Congress are afforded more respect than would be the case if they held lesser offices. Because their work is so important, potentially affecting the lives of literally billions of people worldwide, journalists might be inclined to pay more attention to what representatives say and do than to the color of their skin.

2. *To the extent that we do find racialized media coverage of Congress, what is its cause?* The assumption in most studies is that the media are wholly responsible for racialized coverage. Yet, we do know that some politicians place considerable emphasis on race and racial issues. This emphasis may reflect deeply held values or serve as calculated election-year strategies or possibly some of both. Whatever a politician's motives, if news reports accurately reflect what he or she says and does, then to ask for less racialized news would be to ask for precisely the sort of selective reporting we have earlier criticized. This is an important distinction, as the task of identifying an appropriate remedy for race-dominated news hinges on our ability to identify those responsible for its perseverance.

3. *What are the real-world political effects of racialized reporting?* While we know that watching or reading the news can affect opinions on a variety of issues, there is virtually no evidence showing any direct connection between racialized coverage and citizens' attitudes or behaviors. It is all well and good to postulate about the potential effects of racialized news, but does it really make a difference?

These three questions capture our attention throughout the remainder of the book. In an effort to determine the extent of racialized coverage of Congress, Chapter 2 reports the results of a content analysis of newspaper articles spanning the years 1993 to 1999, noting differences in the way African American and white members of Congress have been portrayed.

Chapter 3 represents the first of our efforts to ferret out the causes of racialized reporting. The chapter opens by recounting the details of interviews with a sample of congressional press secretaries asked to evaluate the media's performance. Of particular note are the significant differences uncovered between press secretaries in white members' offices and those in African American members' offices. The chapter then turns to an analysis of congressional Web sites on the Internet, which provide keen insight into members' interests and priorities. By analyzing these sites, we are able to discern that, in general, African American members do not attempt to portray themselves in a different light than white members.

Chapter 4 turns to the media's version of events. Here, we describe interviews with congressional reporters who were asked to comment on whether they believe race plays a significant role in the way members of Congress are portrayed. Additionally, we examine some of the factors that might influence reporters' evaluations of members of Congress, such as the reporter's own race or the concentration of African American officials in the reporter's geographic area.

In Chapter 5 we consider the effects racialized coverage might have on public opinion and voting behavior. Constituents' evaluations are considered in light of their own race, the race of their representative, and their attentiveness to the news media. Our findings suggest that racialized reporting does have a significant negative effect on the way African American members are perceived by their constituents, particularly white constituents.

The book's final chapter offers a few pragmatic suggestions for improving the quality of congressional media coverage, concluding with a brief blueprint for future research. Although it is surely unrealistic to expect that a single study can somehow undo a well-entrenched formula for news reporting, we hope to shed light on a phenomenon that may prove to be one of the most significant remaining hurdles to racial equality in America.

NOTES

1. Two of the nonvoting delegates in the House are also African American.

2. See, for example, the American Society of Newspaper Editors (ASNE) 1999 report, "Why Newspaper Credibility Has Been Dropping," available at their web site (www.asne.org).

3. Watts, Domke, Shah, and Fan (1999) find that the actual partisan tone of campaign coverage has little to do with perceptions of whether that coverage is fair.

4. Groeling and Kernell (1998) find a version of this problem when they document the greater attention network news programs give to decreases in presidential popularity than to increases in presidential popularity.

5. Actually, the opposite is probably true: media reports are likely to exaggerate the amount of conflict in Congress, leaving citizens to infer that there is more gridlock and petty partisan bickering than is actually the case.

6. See, for example, Stempel 1971; Sentman 1983; Lester and Smith 1990.

7. *Toronto Star*, September 13, 1998.

8. Conyers identifies these issues on his web site (http://www.house.gov/conyers/bio_john_conyers.html).

2

A Choice between Black and White: The Scope of Racialized Coverage of Congress

The language is direct. The distinction is mentioned presumably because it is meaningful and clear. In the *Christian Science Monitor*, the U.S. Senate race between Jesse Helms and Harvey Gantt was described as "a choice between black and white."[1] In fact, papers across the country have described political contests involving African Americans as offering voters the opportunity to "choose between black and white" candidates.[2]

If that is the choice, then the options must be mutually exclusive. Moreover, if that is the choice, then there must be an important distinction between the two.

Does this "important distinction" mean white and African American politicians get different media coverage? Does coverage of white and African Americans in Congress vary consistently and systematically by race? Surely, the media are too fair to allow any bias into their coverage.

To the contrary, most Americans say media coverage is best described as "biased and unfair." In fact, from 1985 to 1998, the media went from eight in ten Americans believing they were fair to eight in ten believing they were unfair.[3]

Most prominent in decrying the media's treatment of African American politicians, though, have been African American politicians (see, e.g., Gibbons 1993; Kleppner 1985; Maisel 1982; Pettigrew and Alston 1988; Clay 1992). Leaders of the Congressional Black Caucus have spoken forcefully and sometimes contemptuously, of the media fixation with race (Gibbons 1993; Maisel 1982; Clay 1992).

Concluding that media coverage is unfair to you or your group is hardly conclusive evidence of bias, of course. In fact, some studies have found people on opposing sides of a controversy, viewing identical coverage, both concluding that coverage was biased against their position (Vallone, Ross, and Lepper 1985). Gunther (1992) finds the tendency to perceive bias is especially strong among those with high involvement, suggesting that politicians themselves and their closest advisers will be least capable of accurately perceiving coverage tendencies.

Significantly, political science and communication researchers in studies on the local, congressional, and national levels have offered affirmation to the claims of African American leaders (e.g., Grainey, Pollack, and Kusmierek 1984; Gibbons 1993; Reeves 1997; Terkildsen 1996; Payne 1988; Barber and Gandy 1990; Chaudhary 1980; Bell 1973).

THE SAMPLE

Importantly, though, much of the academic research in this area has not utilized an adequate comparison sample when analyzing coverage of African Americans. In other words, studies that offer the strongest conclusions about biased coverage of African American political leaders do so without being able to demonstrate how that coverage is actually different from typical coverage of whites.[4] Without a comparison sample of whites' coverage, the shape, style, tone, or amount of coverage of African Americans can hardly be linked to racial bias. Unfortunately, conclusions have often been advanced about the portrayal of African Americans without having a mechanism in place to judge its relative difference.

To understand not just how African Americans in Congress are covered but also how this coverage is different from the portrayals of white members, we compare the treatment of the 1998 class of African American members to the treatment of two groups of their white contemporaries. In the first group, 20 white, male members of Congress whose ideology and tenure in office are similar to those of the African American legislators were selected.[5] This liberal control group was complemented by a second group of 20 white, male members of Congress who are roughly representative of whites in Congress, which is to say, mostly Republican and mostly conservative.[6] Through the use of these three groups of legislators (African Americans, liberal control group, overall control group) the coverage received by African American members can be understood for the degree it reflects something unique to African American legislators, something applicable to liberal legislators, or something common to the range of legislators.

CONTENT ANALYSIS

Media coverage on these members of Congress is assessed with a content analysis of newspaper articles focusing on them from January 1993 to April 1999. For most members in our sample, this time frame represents their entire congressional career to date. Given that some members of our sample have not served for the entire period under study, the data are not intended to afford year-by-year comparisons of coverage. Rather, the data are intended to encapsulate coverage emblematic of the careers of the members under study.

For each member in the sample, articles in which he or she was a primary subject,[7] and that appeared in a "major newspaper"[8] or wire service report were read and analyzed.

We use articles where the member is the focus, not articles that simply mention the member, to allow us sufficient material to analyze. Analyzing all mentions of the members would provide us with copious cases, but because members of Congress are frequently written about in lists — lists of how members voted, for example — those articles leave little room for media colorings and few distinctions to analyze.

We analyze coverage in major newspapers, as opposed to a random sample of newspapers, for three reasons. First, these papers represent the biggest, most widely read publications in the United States. Analyzing this group provides access to the papers Americans are most likely to read. Second, the position of these papers, frequently as the flagship publications of their media group, means their coverage is frequently reprinted in (or, at minimum, influences) smaller papers' stories on Congress.[9] Included in the major newspaper category are also the wire services, such as the Associated Press, which exist to provide nationally used copy. Third, these major papers are the papers of record for the nation, the respected journals of our news that win the Pulitzers and theoretically represent the best of newspaper reporting. Bias found in these papers, therefore, is bias emanating from our most reliable sources, coverage that is likely to be imitated or directly reproduced in countless other papers, in short, coverage that is most likely to reach the American people.

In total, the average member of our sample attracted about seven articles focusing on him or her per year in these major newspapers. For members who attracted ten or fewer articles in a year, we include all of those articles in the analysis. For members who attracted more than ten articles, we randomly chose 20% of the articles for inclusion in the analysis (though never fewer than ten articles were chosen in those cases).

Based on the criticisms from African American politicians and the results of the preliminary studies that have been done (Entman 1992, 1994; Terkildsen 1996; Niven and Zilber 1996; Riffe, Sneed, and Van Ommeren 1989; Grainey, Pollack, and Kusmierek 1984; Gibbons 1993), we examined five attributes of congressional media coverage: amount, racial focus, setting, member importance, and tone.

Amount. Previous research suggests that African Americans might be shut out of some media coverage because the media consider them to be less important or less serious political players (Gibbons 1993). Notably, African American members of Congress, in stark contrast to typical white members who were found to have been quite satisfied with the amount of their media coverage, have lambasted media inattention to their work (Clay 1992; Maisel 1982). Representative Alan Wheat (D-MO) complained that "the media is totally against me"; more specifically, he cited the amount of coverage he received, claiming "there was a total news blackout" on him for years (quoted in Maisel 1982, 117). Ron Dellums (D-CA) took to the floor of the House to decry his media mistreatment: "I have stood with many other progressives on the floor of this Congress. . . . Pick up the newspaper. You never see one word about that, and we wonder why. . . . I dream of the day when many of my colleagues and I can communicate openly with the American people, with no one distorting, no one deciding that Ron Dellums is too radical to quote."[10]

Campbell (1995), studying coverage of race and racial issues, concurs with Wheat and Dellums. Campbell found that the media do not consider African American concerns to be particularly pressing,[11] relevant, or newsworthy; thus, African American leaders may receive less attention.

We examine three indicators of amount of coverage: number of articles focusing on the member, the placement of the articles, and the length of the articles. The three measures offer strong evidence on how prominently the media cover African Americans versus other liberals and how prominently African American members are covered versus members in general.

Racial Focus. A number of studies have concluded that the media reinforce perceptions of differences between whites and African Americans through their peculiar emphasis on African Americans' presumed interest in race (Wilson and Gutierrez 1985; Gibbons 1993; Campbell 1995). Perhaps the most prominent complaint of African American leaders about the media is that reporters cover African American politicians as if racial matters were their only concern.

Jesse Jackson was particularly troubled by the racial obsession of reporters covering his presidential campaigns. To wit, *Newsweek* magazine reporters actually debated whether to bother asking Jackson foreign policy questions because, as primarily a symbolic candidate in their eyes, they doubted that there was any need to hear from him on a full range of issues (Gibbons 1993, xi). This sentiment was summed up nicely by *New York Times* columnist William Safire, who said that Jackson "evidently sees himself as an American black rather than a Black American. Black is not the adjective but the noun — the thing that he is — and leadership of blacks in particular, and not of Americans in general, is his quest. . . . [Jackson] is using the campaign for leadership of blacks in America. In so doing, he expands the total electorate a little and divides it a lot" (quoted in Gibbons 1993, 47).

Jackson lamented that the media labeled his issues "traditional black concerns" rather than what they represented to him, issues of social justice that applied to people regardless of their ethnic background (Gibbons 1993, 65). Jackson noted that despite his nearly universal appellation in the media as the "black Presidential candidate," he never heard a reporter refer to Walter Mondale as the "white Vice President" (Gibbons 1993, 65).

On the congressional level specifically, the Congressional Black Caucus (CBC) has held hearings on what it perceives to be the media's disjointed notions of race. CBC member Alan Wheat's comment represents the general feeling among African American members: "They'll never quote me on anything unless it deals with minorities" (quoted in Maisel 1982, 117).

We consider four measures of racial focus. First, we examine whether the member is depicted as being interested in a racial issue.[12] Second, is the member depicted as being interested in any nonracial issue? Third, is the member's race mentioned? Fourth, is the racial makeup of the member's district mentioned? If African Americans are uniquely being subject to racially focused coverage, their coverage should disproportionately mention racial issues compared with white members, while white members should receive disproportionate attention for their concern on nonracial issues. Further, if race is being used to define these members, mentions of the members' race and the racial makeup of their district should be prominent for African American members but not for white members.

Setting. Some African American leaders have also suggested that the media belittle their work by overemphasizing the local nature of their concerns and efforts. By placing them in their communities, instead of in Washington, such coverage implies that these members are comfortable pandering to the voters but less committed to actually getting their job done. Entman's (1992) work suggests that African American leaders are frequently depicted complaining and agitating but seldom shown getting things done. In the congressional context, such a pattern would place African American members in their districts complaining about what the government is doing wrong, while white members would be more likely to be placed in Washington, working to make things better.

As an indicator of setting, we consider the dateline and whether the text of the article depicts the member in the district, in Washington, or both. If the media are localizing African American representatives, then they should have disproportionately fewer stories datelined or set in Washington.

Importance of Member. Ultimately, members must assert their capacity to get things done. Researchers have suggested that the media often write off African Americans, deriding their capacity to accomplish goals or make a contribution (Martindale and Dunlap 1997). Whether the characterization is one of lack of commitment to the work of legislating or lack of ability to influence fellow legislators, some argue that the media are prone to question the likelihood of African American success (Broh 1987).

We investigate, then, whether the media are more likely to depict African Americans as outsiders to the legislative process and whites as insiders to the process. The distinction is based on the member's capacity to get things done. We define an insider as someone of abnormally high influence, a member who is, for example, depicted as "important," "a leader," "a major voice in the process." An outsider, conversely, is a member who experiences more than the typical frustrations of being one of 435, someone who is portrayed as "locked out of the process," "ignored," "degraded," or "belittled."

Tone. Finally, we consider the overall tone of the coverage. Byrd (1997, 96), then the ombudsman of the *Washington Post*, in a self-study of her own newspaper, found that images of whites in the paper were much more likely to be positive than images of African Americans (19% more images of whites were positive than for African Americans).[13] Following the work of Mondak (1995) and Tidmarch and Pitney (1985), we characterized articles as either negative, neutral, or positive. Positive stories compliment the member's effort, concern, commitment, accomplishments, or intelligence. Negative stories criticize the member in any of those areas. Most stories, Tidmarch and Pitney (1985) find, do neither. That is, in reporting the outcome of congressional events, reporters neither credit nor disparage the membership. Nevertheless, Entman (1994) finds far more negative attention directed toward African American politicians than white politicians.

Impeachment. Given the historic importance as well as the vast media attention to the impeachment of President Bill Clinton, all of these factors are also considered in a separate section that analyzes the portrayal of white and African American members' decisions on impeachment.

The content analysis was performed by a team of four trained coders who each analyzed roughly one-fourth of the 2,524 articles in the sample. The coders were unaware of the expectations that guided the research. A subset of articles analyzed by each coder was analyzed a second time to ensure consistency. On the subjective measures of tone and importance, intercoder reliability was at least .8 for each of the four coders.

The results of the content analysis are encapsulated in Table 2.1. A discussion of the findings and examples of the coverage follow.

AMOUNT OF COVERAGE

The number, length, and placement of articles on African American and white members reveal no major differences between the two groups. African American members garnered about seven articles per year, the liberal comparison sample received about six articles per year, and the overall comparison sample about seven articles per year. Such a difference is not statistically significant.[14] Nor is there a great difference in the length of those articles, with African Americans receiving coverage that is slightly longer than the overall comparison group and slightly less

Table 2.1

Media Coverage of African American and White Members of Congress

	African American	Liberal Comparison	Overall Comparison
Amount of Coverage Articles Per Year	7	6	7
Words per Article	818	822	815
Placement (page number)	8	7	8
Racial Focus Racial Issue	51	11**	6**
Non-Racial Issue	46	82**	86**
Race of Voters	13	5**	4**
Race of Member	41	2**	2**
Setting Washington Dateline	52	62**	61**
Member in Washington	66	71*	74**
Member in District	40	35*	34*
Power Insider	23	26	29*
Outsider	9	3**	1**
Tone Positive	11	24**	28**
Neutral	72	71	67*
Negative	17	5**	5**

N=2524.
Note: Cell entries are percentages, except for the first three rows.
Source: Authors' content analysis of congressional coverage, 1993-1999.
** difference (between group and African American members) significant at p<.01 using 2-tailed T-test.
* difference (between group and African American members) significant at p<.05 using 2-tailed T-test.

than the liberal comparison group.[15] The average placement for African American articles and for the overall sample is page 8, while for liberal comparison samples it is page 7. Neither the differences in length nor placement are statistically significant. With these simple, objective, and meaningful measures of press treatment, we can say that African American and white members of Congress are apparently afforded similar treatment with regard to overall article exposure.

RACIAL TUNNEL VISION

The same cannot be said for the media's attention to race. Coverage of racial issues for white and African American members differs vastly. While the majority of articles on African American members mention a racial issue, only 11% of the articles on the liberal sample and barely 6% of the articles on the overall sample mention racial issues. The same pattern is repeated with regard to mentions of the member's race: 41% of the articles identify the race of African American members, and only 2% of the articles on the comparison samples identify those members as white. The race of the voters is also more likely to be mentioned in articles on African Americans, as 13% of the articles on African American members mention the racial makeup of district voters, while 5% and 4% of the articles on the liberal and overall comparison groups, respectively, mention the race of their constituents. The reverse pattern, not surprisingly, exists for coverage of nonracial issues, where more than eight out of ten articles on the overall and liberal comparison groups mention a nonracial issue, but less than half of the articles on African Americans mention their interest in nonracial issues.

The ubiquity of racial mentions in coverage of African Americans is so strong as to almost be unrecognized and unremarkable. Louis Stokes (D-OH) is consistently, as if it is part of his name, "Ohio's first and only black Congressman,"[16] Harold Ford (D-TN) is "Tennessee's only black member of Congress,"[17] James Clyburn (D-SC) is "the first black to represent South Carolina in Congress since Reconstruction."[18] Admittedly, Clyburn is sometimes referred to differently, for example, as "the first African American to represent South Carolina in Congress since Reconstruction."[19] Lest we not have complete understanding of their position on the African American roll call, the *Sacramento Bee* informs us that Eva Clayton (D-NC) and Melvin Watt (D-NC) are "the first blacks elected to Congress from North Carolina this century"; however, they are not the "first post-1901 blacks to be elected to Congress from the Old Confederacy. That honor fell to Barbara Jordan, in 1971."[20]

In one article on Donald Payne (D-NJ) (aka "the first and only black Congressman from New Jersey"), the *Pittsburgh Post-Gazette* refers to Representative Payne as being black or being associated with blacks an impressive 11 times.[21]

The simplest explanation for this racially loaded coverage pattern is rather benign. Perhaps this coverage is merely a reflection of what members talk about, care about, and act on, and is thus a reflection of how members present themselves. Closer examination of the coverage suggests the process may not be that simple — and that reporters may inject race into stories on African American members regardless of those members' priorities.

Coverage of the crime bill of 1994 is such a case. According to the *Houston Chronicle*'s coverage, African American members of Congress were hostile to the bill because of its effects on the African American community. One article states, "Many [Congressional Black] caucus members say they fear the bill's get tough provisions will unfairly target black defendants. They also are unhappy at the failure of the racial justice act that would allow a black person convicted of murder to challenge a death sentence if it seemed that race influenced the sentencing process."[22]

Despite the clear conclusion that African American members based their reaction to this bill on its effects on African American constituents, nothing in the statements of African American members that the paper referred to supports this claim. In fact, when Earl Hilliard (D-AL) said he was against the crime bill because of its expansion of the death penalty, his reasoning was: "I just don't like sending 13 year-olds to the electric chair."[23] Other African American members, including Charles Rangel (D-NY), said they opposed the bill because it did not do enough to get guns off the streets.[24] Thus, the paper makes this a racial issue when the members themselves advanced no racial argument on the matter.

Contrast this approach with the coverage received by white member Maurice Hinchey (D-NY) on this same bill. Hinchey, speaking to what was billed as a "predominantly black audience," discussed his position on the crime bill without the reporter's offering the slightest implication that Hinchey's position was based on race or that his answers focused on race.[25] White and African American members can have the same stance on the same issue, with the white member appearing in a setting where the coverage might logically be tilted toward race, and yet the white member has a well-thought-out and inclusive position, while the African American member has a racially based position.

Time and again, African American members are portrayed as having exclusive concern about the African American community. Bennie Thompson (D-MS), in the words of a *Baton Rouge Advocate* reporter, came to town to discuss "problems that plague *the black Mississippian*."[26] Thompson, in his own words, said his goal was far different: "I'm hoping that the sessions will help us formulate a plan to better the future for *all* of us."[27] John Lewis (D-GA) spoke at an event celebrating the 35th anniversary of Martin Luther King Jr.'s "I Have a Dream Speech."[28] While the event and speech were predictably written up as dealing exclusively with civil rights and racial issues, the actual words of Representative Lewis were much more inclusive: "We all came over here on different ships, but we all live in the same boat now." In story after story, the media take the inclusive concerns of African American representatives that suggest our fundamental similarities and portray these leaders as having exclusive concerns that suggest our fundamental differences (see also Entman 1994).

As Jesse Jackson suggested earlier, when he speaks of poverty, the media hear "African American poverty." His concern is the poor of all ethnicities and backgrounds, but the media fractionalize his commitment. Similarly, for these African American members, their concerns may know no racial boundaries, but their portrayal suggests they hardly think of anything but race.

Interestingly, reporters occasionally take note of the potentially damaging and unrealistic tendency to define members of Congress too narrowly. A *Washington Post* article noted: "It's insane. A guy goes to Congress to work on health care, Social Security, Trade, hundreds of meaningful things, and some folks wind up ignoring the total and shrinking the guy's net worth to one issue."[29] That defense, however, was of a white member, James Moran (D-VA).

When race does come up in coverage of white members, it is often in the context of controversy over words rather than deeds. Gerald Solomon (R-NY) publicly stated that United Nations secretary-general Kofi Annan (of Ghana) "ought to be horsewhipped." Donald Payne called the comment a "racist insult," highlighting "the painful image of a black person being whipped into submission by his master."[30]

One of the more noted exchanges on race involving white members came when Patrick Kennedy (D-RI) verbally sparred with Bob Barr (R-

GA) in the hallway outside the House chamber. Barr suggested members should follow the example of John F. Kennedy's *Profiles in Courage* when casting their impeachment votes.

Patrick Kennedy, the New York *Daily News* reported, said to Barr:

"You're the same man to meet with a white supremacist group. Anybody who has been to a racist crowd like that has no right invoking my uncle's memory, I'll tell you that."

"You're wrong," Barr shot back. "First of all, you're wrong to interject that sort of lack of decorum into these halls."

"I'm not on the floor now, Mr. Barr."

"I'm well aware of where you are. You have a problem with it?" Barr said. "Young man, you just say what you like."

"I have a problem with it. I am a duly elected member of my state. Calling me a young man . . ." Kennedy said indignantly, his left hand shaking.

"Oh, I'm impressed," Barr said sarcastically. "I'm duly impressed."[31]

The *Atlanta Journal and Constitution* reported that Kennedy later said, "It appalled me that a racist would invoke my uncle's name. We ought to be very clear where Mr. Barr is coming from. He is a racist and a liar."[32] While Barr replied: "To have some punk accuse me of being a racist is absolutely disgusting. I don't know if he's gone off the deep end or what."[33]

Thus, added to the general dearth of white members discussing matters relating to race are these semantic squabbles that serve to further undermine the importance of African American concerns and further isolate the white member from the African American member. When issues of race are reduced to fussiness over words, the practical effect to some is to suggest that there are no real grievances (Smith 1992), nothing substantive at stake, and consequently the issues are on the level of trivia and minutiae (Keever 1997). The argument over whether one member has insulted another is a debate that will not feed anyone, clothe anyone, or change the marginal tax rate.

Whites are shown making few policy pronouncements on race. As Representative William Clay (D-MO) puts it, "white members of Congress are never expected to speak out on controversial race incidents where white mobs have attacked black citizens or white police officers have butchered non-white citizens."[34] When whites do receive coverage on racial matters, their petty squabbling serves only to underscore the lack of importance of the issue area to white members.

Overwhelmingly, when white representatives are depicted, they are not speaking to racial issues — and that means neither issues that affect only African Americans nor issues that affect only whites. Instead, their concerns are depicted as big-picture concerns, issues that affect everyone (Entman 1994; Campbell 1995). This dichotomy in the coverage between white and African American representatives has the consequence of suggesting that African American politicians think only of their own, while whites care about everybody.

This coverage obviously has serious potential ramifications for African American representatives. A. Lee Parks, a white resident of Georgia who sued to overturn the boundary lines of the majority-African American district his hometown was placed in, explained to the *New York Times* that he sued because African American representatives are "communicating that they prefer their black constituents, that their priority is serving their black constituents. Often that's what polarizes elections on racial lines."[35]

Ironically, that quote appears in an article in which Parks' representative, Sanford Bishop (D-GA), an African American, asserts how little attention he pays to race. Bishop was quoted as saying that "the majority vote their pocketbooks. They understand the precarious situation that the farming community is in and they'll support people that help them," to explain why many whites had supported his reelection.

Bishop's assertion notwithstanding, the article continually mentions Bishop's race and seeks white voter reaction to it.

Ten years ago, Wayne Williams, a peanut farmer here, would no more have considered voting for a black man for Congress than he would have planted his crop in the chill of December. Many of Mr. Bishop's white supporters acknowledge they had to overcome deep prejudices to vote for him. "I just wouldn't have thought a black man would know enough to do the job," Mr. Williams explained. Other white farmers referred to the Congressman matter-of-factly with the coarsest racial epithets before explaining what it was they liked so much about him.[36]

Another white farmer concluded that Bishop's commitment to farm issues was all that mattered to him: "I think most of us have gotten beyond the white and black issue. We prefer to focus on the green."[37]

Inexplicably, in the face of Bishop's comments and those of the voters, the reporter concludes that Bishop is popular because of "his influence — particularly with other black Democrats in the House."[38] The representative said this was not about race, the voters interviewed said this was not about race, even the man who sued because he thought Sanford Bishop was only interested in race conceded that that was not the case. Nevertheless, in the face of both evidence and logic to the contrary, the article concludes that the future of Sanford Bishop, representative of a rural farming community, rides on his relationship with other African Americans. Nothing in the article suggests this; nothing in reality suggests this. However, when you define politics by race, then you better have a racial explanation for your politics.

The Exception that Proves the Rule

To the extent that any current representative would be exempt from the media's typical definitions of African American political leadership, it would likely be Oklahoma's J. C. Watts Jr., the only African American Republican in the House.

Instead of this partisan difference enabling Watts to be viewed outside the strictures of racial stereotypes, his race is all the more noteworthy to reporters. The *Baltimore Sun* pointed out the apparent contradiction between Watts' position in the Republican House leadership and the involvement of a number of prominent Republicans in the racist Council of Conservative Citizens (CCC) organization. The *Sun* went on to point out that Watts' position did not attract African American voters:

To the chagrin of the Republican Party, its elevation of its lone black Congressman, Oklahoma Rep. J.C. Watts, to a leadership position did little to move other African Americans into the GOP fold. Instead, the party was criticized for exercising a type of the same affirmative action it usually opposes.[39]

It is almost as if Watts, as an African American Republican, is not a real member of the House. Democrats not only have been CCC members, but have also been Ku Klux Klan (KKK) members, but that contradiction is presumably not newsworthy because African American members in the Democratic Party are where they belong.

The same newspaper printed a feature on Watts in which the author observed of Watts that: "his skin is black, but oh! His politics are

white."[40] Granted, partisans are apt to criticize those they disagree with —
thus, J. C. Watts Sr., the Oklahoma representative's father and lifelong
Democrat, proclaimed, "I'm not like my boy. . . . I told him that voting for
the Republican ticket is like the chicken voting for Colonel Sanders"[41] —
but the media have no stake in Watts' success or failure.

Like many of his colleagues on the Democratic side of the aisle, Watts
himself does not define politics in terms of race. Instead, he faults the
Republican Party for not reaching out to all voters:

We've got to get serious about outreach. . . . I've been beating my head against the
wall on that for four years. We've got to get more market share. You can't just
throw mud on the wall 60 days before an election and pray some of it sticks; You
have to have a plan that says, 'Here's my view of the future, and it includes you.[42]

Reaction to Watts is so intense and so far from his own presentation
that one is tempted to conclude that the media operate with a standard of
what a white representative is and what an African American representative is. Watts, whose politics defy those conventions, is the square
peg that must be pounded into the round hole.

AT HOME IN THE DISTRICT

Since African American representatives are portrayed as fixated on
matters relating to race, it is not surprising that their coverage is
considerably more locally centered. In other words, the African American
agenda, as portrayed by the media, is one in which the members' goals and
priorities are shaped, and can be viewed best, from within the district.
Coverage of African Americans, the data reveal, is less likely to be set in
Washington (articles on whites were about 10% more likely to have a
Washington dateline, while liberals and the overall comparison sample
were 5% and 8%, respectively, more likely to have their coverage mention
activities in Washington) and more likely to mention the members in their
own districts (40% of coverage of African Americans places them in their
district, compared to 35% of liberal group coverage and 34% of the
overall group's coverage).

Again, this coverage serves to suggest that the agenda of the African
American representative is particularistic and selfish, while the concerns
of the white representative are universal and selfless. While it is common
to find articles that place African Americans' priorities in their district, it

is considerably more difficult to find instances in which their coverage suggests wider interests. Thus, for every African American local story (African American Louis Stokes was noted for his "largesse last year" in securing for his district "$12 million for a new parking garage at the veterans hospital that will bear his name"[43]), there are stories of white members whose depth of knowledge and concern are so great that their districts cannot sufficiently contain their ideas. Read the papers, and you will find Maurice Hinchey of New York fighting to save 6 million acres of wilderness in Utah,[44] Neil Abercrombie (D) of Hawaii making headlines by securing funding to save the Asian elephant,[45] and Washington state's Jim McDermott (D) meeting with Florida business leaders to work on proposals to make small business health insurance more affordable.[46]

This coverage, of course, is not inherently detrimental to African American representatives. Concern for one's district is certainly a hallmark of congressional service, and members expend considerable effort convincing their constituents that they are hard at work on the district's behalf (Fenno 1978). At the level of the prospective voter in a home district, the typical coverage African Americans receive may be highly valuable.

Nevertheless, this pattern is significant for two reasons. First, concern for their district can hardly be restricted to African Americans, leaving the media again in the position of attending to, and probably exaggerating, differences between white and African American members. Second, this distinction implies that African Americans' narrow concerns are the result of ethnic selfishness rather than vision, a daunting portrayal if the member should wish to seek higher office or must face a redrawn district that includes significant numbers of white voters.[47] For these voters, it is the white representative who speaks for everyone and thus for them, while the African American representative speaks only for African Americans.

"GNAT ON THE ELEPHANT'S HIDE"

African American leaders are concerned with their own group and focused on their own district. However, their concerns are not listened to on Capitol Hill with equal vigor. African American members are 6% less likely than the overall comparison sample to be portrayed as being Capitol Hill insiders capable of accomplishing what they want. More startling, they are nine times more likely than the overall sample to be portrayed as

Capitol Hill outsiders, incapable of making things happen and often incapable of commanding even a modicum of respect.

While white members such as Gene Green (D-TX) have so much clout that they are continually bringing Clinton administration officials to visit with the folks back home,[48] African American members such as Cynthia McKinney (D-GA) cannot even get past the front gate when trying to visit the White House. McKinney, according to press accounts, was ignored by a White House guard, who eventually spoke to McKinney's white aide but not to her.[49] While white member Ted Strickland (D-OH) is "persuading" the president to do what he wants,[50] African American members "toil amid adversity."[51] While white member Maurice Hinchey's proposals will "sail through the House,"[52] African American members are sitting by while their political power has "dramatically eroded,"[53] leaving them holding all the influence of a "gnat on the elephant's hide."[54]

While white member Jerry Costello (D-IL) celebrates his "certain" support from the president for a Costello bill,[55] African American member William Clay appears at another "sparsely attended news conference."[56] Clay was further mocked because the press conference he had called was bogged down by another representative "who rambled on and on," while Clay sat impassively. Instead of asserting himself, "Clay fidgeted, looking at his watch."[57]

As the overall coverage of white and African American members suggests they have a significantly different level of power, side-by-side comparisons in the same articles offer similar perspectives. In an article on the New York congressional delegation, the *Daily News* specifically christens African American member Major Owens (D) as the least influential member of Congress in the New York City area.[58] The article, which included both House members and senators, anointed Al D'Amato (R), who would be defeated in his bid for reelection nine months later, as the best member of the delegation. In a *Sacramento Bee* article on the retirements of Ron Dellums and Vic Fazio (D-CA), Dellums, an African American, is deemed "not a political mover and shaker," while Fazio, who is white, used "his position to increase his influence with other members in both parties."[59] Notable in this article is that the paper's conclusions contradict various lobbyists and lawmakers cited in the piece who considered the loss of Dellums to be at least as significant as the retirement of Fazio.

While in many cases the media constructed their own opinion and portrayal of the African American member as a weak outsider, they also gave significant attention to instances in which other lawmakers appeared to compromise the dignity of an African American representative. When African American representative Sheila Jackson-Lee (D-TX) appeared as a guest of another Democratic lawmaker at a subcommittee for which she was not a member, the *New York Times* wrote that the Republican subcommittee chair's "plangent expression posed another question, which went unspoken: Would she please just go away?"[60] After referring to Jackson-Lee as "Congress's resident noodge,"[61] the article notes that when Jackson-Lee was offered the chance to speak at the hearing, her Democratic colleagues "groaned."

As Broh (1987) has argued, in the media's view of the world, African American leaders are supposed to think with one mind on every subject. Thus, disagreements between African Americans are not only notable but worthy of dramatic phrasing. African American leaders do not disagree; they "feud."[62] They do not have opponents; they have "enemies."[63] Feuds are activities for the unrefined and the powerless. Having enemies is the stuff of childhood, not a mark of distinguished political leadership and diplomacy.

To be clear, this portrayal of African American powerlessness is not merely a reflection of their position in the minority party. The numbers reveal that white Democrats, who, since the 1994 election, have been locked out of power along with African American representatives, are significantly less likely to be portrayed as outsiders than African Americans. To wit, white Democrat Peter Deutsch (FL) was profiled in the *Washington Post* in 1998 suggesting that the Democrats were working together better than they had in 16 years,[64] while African Americans were fumbling around helpless even to extract the barest indication of remorse from a Republican who called the President a "scumbag." The incident prompted Major Owens to conclude that "never has the Congress sunk to lower depths."[65]

While not quantifiable, the evocative imagery of African American powerlessness adds to its significance. It is African American members who are said to lack the influence even of a "gnat on the elephant's hide." It is the African American member of Congress who cannot move about the Capitol building without being accosted by security personnel, according to media write-ups.[66] It is the African American member who is reported to have had a more attentive audience when he preached sermons to his family's chickens as a boy than he has now when he speaks in the U.S. House of Representatives.[67]

THE TONE OF COVERAGE

Consistent with previous research (Tidmarch and Pitney 1985), the majority of articles on members of Congress are neutral in tone. For both African American and white members, the typical article neither compliments them nor derides them.

Nevertheless, there is a great difference in the ratio of positive to negative articles. For white members, there are five positive articles for every negative article. For African Americans, the ratio is less than one positive article for every negative article.

Entman (1994) suggests the grave potential consequences for this pattern, as African American officials are already the numerical exception, which, when combined with the greater negative coverage they receive, can serve to create a strong association between the majority traits (white, positive) and the minority traits (African American, negative). Psychologists call this the problem of illusory correlation (Fiske and Taylor 1991, 373-376). The illusory correlation here could result in an assumption that white members are good and African Americans bad, even though the vast majority of both are not receiving negative coverage (see Hamilton and Gifford 1976).

Among the most notable contrasts in coverage of white and African American members is the portrayal of hard work and commitment. Common in features on white members are comments such as: Martin Meehan (D-MA) "maintains a listed [home] telephone number (978-454-1674) and as many as three dozen of his constituents make use of it daily,"[68] "Gene Green says he tries to return every constituent's telephone call,"[69] Ted Strickland "works hard at the minutiae of constituent service."[70] African Americans are seldom complimented for their dedication and more apt to feel the scorn of reporters, as did William Clay, who "feels no obligation to explain his whereabouts, to reporters or anyone else."[71]

White members do not just work harder; they are more pleasant and down to earth while on the job. For a white member, praise for showing up and meeting voters: "There, at 9:30 A.M., Jim Moran ambled in, absolutely on time, no Praetorian guard fronting him and no flunkie trailing him. He'd driven himself. Skilled at the art, he commenced schoomzing the room, a meeting hall in the Mason District Government Center in Fairfax County."[72] An African American member is much more likely to be disagreeable, as Sheila Jackson-Lee is "so rude to flight attendants" that airlines no longer want her as a customer, such an "imperious taskmaster" that she has "quicksilver turnover" among staff,[73] so truculent that, metaphorically, she could not foster an agreement with Republicans "on whether to bag with paper or plastic at the supermarket."[74]

Flaws in their approach to the job also prominently include African Americans' lack of independent thought and action. It is African American members, not white members, who are portrayed as reliable followers of the House Democratic leadership[75] and African American members who will consistently follow the president's lead.[76] This characterization is made despite the fact that there are at least 100 white Democrats in the House of whom the same could be said. Nonetheless, while white members "persuade" the president, African American members are persuaded by him.

Even in the rare instances in which an African American member initially disagrees with President Clinton, the media portray African Americans as ultimately powerless to resist the president's wishes. In an article on the 1994 crime bill, the *Houston Chronicle* quoted Earl Hilliard as saying the president's lobbying of opponents of the bill, like himself, was very engaging. The headline of the article was taken directly from Hilliard's words: "I must say the guy is good."[77] What the article did not emphasize, mention in the headline, or reveal until the middle of the story was that despite Hilliard's compliments, he continued to oppose the president's position.

In the picture painted by the media, African American members appear less likely to work hard, think hard, or approach the job correctly. For African Americans, negativity suggests an uncomfortablity or incompatibility with the job. White members, conversely, enjoy a portrayal that often suggests they were made for the work. It is the white member, in this case Bart Stupak (D-MI), who is happy, hard-charging, and known to say, "I love my job."[78]

RACE AND IMPEACHMENT

According to the results of the content analysis, African Americans' coverage heavily emphasizes race, suggests they have a parochial focus and little influence in Washington, and implies they are less well suited for the job.

Did these patterns persist in the media's coverage of the impeachment process? The significance of the question is threefold. First, this is an issue that dominated the headlines of 1998 and early 1999 and therefore was a major component of media coverage of Congress. Second, for many members, this was a development that was by far "the most important vote" they have ever taken during their congressional service.[79] Accordingly, members felt that to the extent any vote was crucial and would define their political careers, this was it. Third, this issue has nothing inherently to do with race. Therefore, if similar patterns occur in coverage of impeachment, it powerfully reinforces the ubiquity of racialized coverage of Congress.

According to the media, African Americans in the House were "Clinton loyalists,"[80] "supporters who have not wavered from the president."[81] African Americans offered "unwavering support,"[82] "friendship,"[83] and were Clinton's "chief defenders"[84] throughout the impeachment process.

No problem here, the media might assert. African Americans in the House were, after all, largely opponents of impeachment. The problem, though, is that the caricature that is applied to African Americans again suggests they think alike, rather than for themselves. They are, these words suggest, controlled by the president.

Consider Sheila Jackson-Lee, who was characterized during the impeachment process as both a "Clinton defender" and an "outspoken Clinton partisan."[85] How did Jackson-Lee establish her loyalty? What was her position? Ironically, she was a leading voice calling for a censure resolution against the president.

African American members, by and large, did not defend the president. Instead, they consistently called for a fair process.

Donald Payne: President Clinton deserves fair treatment. . . . There should not be a rush to judgement.[86]

Sheila Jackson-Lee: We don't turn away from fundamental fairness.[87]

Major Owens: It is of the utmost importance that we acknowledge and support the spirit of our Constitution.[88]

In the media's depiction, white Democrats, in contrast to the ill-considered positions of African Americans, "agonized" over what should be done.[89] White Democrats, again in contrast to their African American colleagues, were not "Clinton loyalists"; rather, they were merely "opposed to Impeachment"[90] and offered "a balance to the shrill partisanship."[91]

Incredibly, the same article that portrays white Democrat Ken Bentsen (D-TX) as having a balanced position and taking a "wait and see" approach to impeachment, calls Sheila Jackson-Lee a "front and center defender" of the president.[92] The difference in their positions? While Jackson-Lee favored censure of the president, Bentsen, on the other hand, favored censure of the president.

Jackson-Lee, here portrayed as sweetly smitten with the president, is the same woman who is out of control and domineering to those around her. It seems the portrayal of Jackson-Lee neatly conforms to reporters' predispositions, without regard for their apparent contradictions.

When Democrats gathered together during the impeachment process to meet with President Clinton, the media covered the events with glowing terms. "Clinton gets warm welcome from House Democrats," who greeted him with "a standing ovation so prolonged that he had to motion for members to sit down."[93] Or, Clinton and House Democrats created a "jubilant and united front."[94] What this coverage has in common, though, is consistently turning first to African American members to explain the party's support of Clinton. Despite making up less than one-fifth of the Democratic caucus, it is as if these jubilant meetings with prolonged standing ovations reflected the support only of African Americans.

In perhaps the definitive example of the media tendency to exaggerate the role of race, the *Washington Post* published an article on the five members of the House who voted against any form of an impeachment investigation. These five Democrats were John Lewis, Cynthia McKinney, Jose Serrano (NY), Bob Filner (CA), and Paul Kanjorski (PA). Of the five, Lewis and McKinney are African American, Serrano is Latino, and Filner and Kanjorski are white. Two African Americans, two whites, one Latino take a rather unique position on an issue, and the *Post*'s explanation for their position, despite offering no support from any of the five members involved or any evidence whatsoever, is that these five members were linked by the "large concentration of minority voters" in their districts.[95] Were the *Post* staff to visit Kanjorski's district looking for that large concentration of minorities they believe resides there, they would find the task rather challenging, as fully 98% of the people Kanjorski represents are white.[96]

Even in an area that has nothing particularly to do with race, the media affix a racial explanation to it. African Americans are of one mind and offer an ill-considered position on impeachment, regardless of the actual facts involved. It does not matter if you favor censure, and it does not matter if white Democrats are behaving similarly; African Americans arrive at the positions they take because they are African Americans, with all the associated unique and racially motivated concerns.

SUMMARY AND CONCLUSION

We examined over six years of newspaper coverage of African American and white members of the House of Representatives. We find that African American and white members receive similar quantities of coverage, but that is where the similarities end.

Compared to a sample of liberal members, as well as a sample of members who reflect the makeup of whites in the House, African American members are vastly more likely to be featured concerning themselves with matters of race and vastly more likely to have their own race and the racial makeup of their districts mentioned.

The implication that African American members care only about their own ethnic group is buttressed by the greater likelihood that African Americans will be portrayed in their district, rather than working in Washington. While in Washington, African Americans will be less likely to get things done, anyway, according to the media.

Thus, African Americans are the subject of less positive and more negative stories than white members. As Entman (1994) found in his study of network news, the overwhelming tendency of the media is to define African Americans as being different, as being a 'them' to the white person's 'us.'[97] Not only are African American representatives not an us, but also they are a group the media suggest are simply less acquitted for this line of work.

We find, in short, that coverage of Congress is racialized, suffused with attention to race and exaggerated distinctions between the races.

Our method of study allows us to address some common concerns about the origins of this coverage. Is this pattern of coverage simply a reflection of media reaction to, or the practical realities of, the fact that most African American members are strongly liberal? No, it is not. Coverage of African Americans is contrasted with coverage of white liberals and is consistently different in terms of racial focus, setting, and tone.

Is this pattern of coverage a reflection of the fact that African Americans, for most of the time under study, were in the minority party and therefore less likely to be powerful? Again such a suggestion is contradicted by the treatment of the white liberals, who also went from the majority party to the minority party. Moreover, a previous study we conducted (Niven and Zilber 1996) suggests the same patterns existed when the Democrats were in the majority.

Ultimately, the pattern of racialized coverage is very consistent with the damning conclusion of Miller's (1977) study on the overall reliability of congressional media coverage. Miller wrote that "journalists tend to impose their own ideas about 'significance' upon an institution and its members, rather than responding to the range of activities underway in that institution and members' relative involvement in these activities" (1977, 465).

Is there, though, something specific to the media priorities of African American members that is conducive to differences in coverage? Do African American members in some way seek press coverage or encourage press coverage in ways that are significantly different from the ways of white members? Perhaps these racialized differences in coverage, or some of these differences, can be explained by the procedures and priorities of African American members' media efforts. We consider these questions in Chapter 3.

NOTES

1. *Christian Science Monitor*, October 29, 1990.

2. For example, *Palm Beach Post*, August 30, 1998; *San Antonio Express-News*, October 30, 1997; *Los Angeles Times*, October 10, 1995.

3. *USA TODAY*, December 16, 1998; *San Francisco Chronicle*, August 1, 1998.

4. For example, neither Gibbons (1993), who studied racialized campaign coverage of Jesse Jackson's presidential campaigns, nor Reeves (1997), who studied racialized campaign coverage of mayoral races, makes an attempt to compare coverage of elections involving African American candidates with elections involving only white candidates. Barber and Gandy (1990) do use a comparison sample in their study of coverage of African American members of Congress, but their comparison group comprises only liberal whites.

5. Both groups have a median year elected of 1992. The African American legislators have an average American for Democratic Action (ADA) ideology score of 87 (0=most conservative, 100=most liberal), while the comparison group has an average ADA of 86. Members in the liberal comparison sample are Martin Meehan (D-MA), Maurice Hinchey (D-NY), Gene Green (D-TX), Thomas Barrett (D-WI), Peter Deutsch (D-FL), Ted Strickland (D-OH), Jim McDermott (D-WA), Frank Pallone (D-NJ), Neil Abercrombie (D-HI), Jerry Costello (D-IL), Patrick

Kennedy (D-RI), Jim Moran (D-VA), Sherrod Brown (D-OH), Earl Pomeroy (D-ND), Jerrod Nadler (D-NY), David Minge (D-MN), Bart Stupak (D-MI), John Olver (D-MA), and Eliot Engel (D-NY).

6. In 1998 about 60% of white males in Congress were Republicans; therefore 60% of this comparison sample are Republicans. The sample was chosen to mirror the experience and ideology of white males in the House. Both the population and the sample have a median year elected of 1992, while the ADA score for the population and the sample are 31 and 33, respectively. Members of the overall control group are Stephen Horn (R-CA), Bob Franks (R-NJ), Jack Quinn (R-NY), Michael Castle (R-DE), Spencer Bachus (R-AL), John Mica (R-FL), Mac Collins (R-GA), Michael Crapo (R-ID), Joe Knollenberg (R-MI), Bob Inglis (R-SC), Bob Goodlatte (R-VA), Donald Manzullo (R-IL), Paul McHale (D-PA), Cal Dooley (D-CA), Collin Peterson (D-MN), Robert Andrews (D-NJ), Chet Edwards (D-TX), Tim Roemer (D-IN), James Barcia (D-MI), and Ron Klink (D-PA).

7. Defined as being mentioned in the headline or in one of the three lead paragraphs of an article.

8. "Major newspapers" is a designation used by the Nexis newspaper search index. It includes national newspapers, as well as larger regional newspapers.

9. The resulting effect is that prominent "inner ring" newspapers and smaller "outer ring" newspapers have a very similar political issue focus (Shaw and Sparrow 1999).

10. *Congressional Record*, June 14, 1978.

11. One of the most gripping examples of the lack of newsworthiness of African American concerns was documented in the *Chicago Journalism Review* (December 1972) — which pointed out that one Chicago daily's coverage of a scientific conference placed an article on the dangers of lead paint to dogs ("Lead Toxic to Puppies") on top of, and with a bigger headline than an article on the threat of lead paint to African American children ("Blacks Prone to Lead Poisoning").

12. We define "racial issue" as it has been used in previous research (e.g., Entman 1992) to mean an issue with a distinct and direct effect on African Americans or a special symbolic significance to African Americans. Issues with a direct effect include affirmative action, while matters of symbolic importance include the designation of holidays, medals, and public recognition for African Americans.

13. In an interesting research test, Rainville and McCormick (1977) document that sports announcers' comments on white and African American football players vary notably, with whites receiving more praise and being less apt to be criticized for their past.

14. Using $p<.05$ in a 2-tailed T-test as the standard.

15. This and all subsequent numbers are weighted to account for the sampling procedure used to select articles for the highly covered members.

16. *USA TODAY*, December 15, 1998.

17. *New York Times*, August 2, 1996.

18. *Boston Globe*, November 18, 1998.

19. *Sacramento Bee*, November 18, 1998.

20. *Sacramento Bee*, December 9, 1995.

21. *Pittsburgh Post-Gazette*, February 18, 1996.

22. *Houston Chronicle*, August 18, 1994.

23. Ibid.

24. Ibid.

25. *Albany Times-Union*, October 30, 1994.

26. *Baton Rouge Advocate*, January 11, 1999.

27. Ibid.

28. *Atlanta Journal and Constitution*, August 28, 1998.

29. *Washington Post*, October 29, 1998.

30. *Buffalo News*, April 8, 1998.

31. *Daily News* (New York), December 19, 1998.

32. *Atlanta Journal and Constitution*, December 19, 1998.

33. Ibid.

34.. Correspondence with authors, September 29, 1999.

35. *New York Times*, December, 30, 1998.

36. Ibid.

37. *New York Times*, December, 30, 1998.

38. *New York Times*, December, 30, 1998.

39. *Baltimore Sun*, December 29, 1998.

40. *Baltimore Sun*, December 10, 1998.

41. *Buffalo News*, November 23, 1998.

42. *New York Times*, November 8, 1998.

43. *Cleveland Plain Dealer*, October 7, 1998.

44. *Salt Lake Tribune*, May 3, 1996.

45. *Washington Post*, June 17, 1997.

46. *Seattle Times*, August 8, 1998.

47. Entman (1992) found white political leaders were more likely to be featured speaking to the wider public interest (as opposed to a narrow ethnic group interest) by a factor of 10 compared to African American political leaders.

48. *Houston Chronicle*, October 24, 1995.

49. *New York Times*, May 9, 1998.

50. *Columbus Dispatch*, December 13, 1998.

51. *Pittsburgh Post-Gazette*, February 18, 1996.

52. *Salt Lake Tribune*, July 23, 1998.

53. *Sacramento Bee*, September 3, 1998.

54. *Atlanta Journal and Constitution*, November 20, 1994.

55. *St. Louis Post Dispatch*, June 4, 1998.

56. *St. Louis Post-Dispatch*, May 19, 1997.

57. Ibid.
58. *Daily News* (New York), February 20, 1998.
59. *Sacramento Bee*, November 19, 1997.
60. *New York Times*, March 8, 1999.
61. Ibid.
62. *New York Times*, January 30, 1999.
63. *Daily News* (New York), August 27, 1998.
64. *Washington Post*, February 13, 1998.
65. *Daily News* (New York), April 24, 1998.
66. *Los Angeles Times*, April 26, 1996.
67. *Daily News* (New York), January 19, 1999.
68. *Boston Globe*, September 13, 1998.
69. *Houston Chronicle*, December 15, 1998.
70. *New York Times*, September 8, 1998.
71. *St. Louis Post-Dispatch*, May 19, 1997.
72. *Washington Post*, October 29, 1998.
73. *New York Times*, March 8, 1999.
74. *Houston Chronicle*, December 13, 1998.
75. *Pittsburgh Post-Gazette*, February 18, 1996.
76. *Houston Chronicle*, March 7, 1999.
77. *Houston Chronicle*, August 18, 1994.
78. *Detroit News*, September 10, 1997.
79. *New York Times*, January 29, 1999; *Boston Globe*, December 14, 1998; *Columbus Dispatch*, December 13, 1998; *Washington Post*, December 16, 1998.
80. Associated Press, September 14, 1998.
81. Associated Press, September 18, 1998.
82. *Newsday*, September 11, 1998.
83. *Kansas City Star*, December 19, 1998.
84. *Milwaukee Journal*, January 19, 1999.
85. *Baltimore Sun*, October 9, 1998.
86. *Newsday*, September 11, 1998.
87. Ibid.
88. Ibid.
89. *Cleveland Plain-Dealer*, December 15, 1998.
90. *Boston Globe*, December 11, 1998.
91. *Milwaukee Journal*, December 27, 1998.
92. *Houston Chronicle*, December 13, 1998.
93. *St. Louis Post-Dispatch*, August 6, 1998.
94. *USA TODAY*, March 4, 1999.
95. *Washington Post*, October 10, 1998.
96. Barone and Ujifusa 1997, 1228.

97. Entman's research (1994) found only 1% of the stories on network news presented African Americans in neutral, 'we're all the same' imagery.

3

Does Race Affect How Members Sell Themselves? A View from the Hill

According to some critics, members of Congress crave positive media attention so wantonly that rather than scrutinizing their legislative agenda to see if it meets the needs of the media, they are more apt to examine their media agenda to see what legislative ideas it holds. Cook (1989) finds a preoccupation with the media such that hardly any decision is made without concern for the media's interest and likely angle on the story.

The question is, in light of the racialized coverage documented in Chapter 2, whether the images of themselves that members are desperately trying to sell vary by the race of the member. Do whites focus on different aspects of themselves and their legislative careers than do African Americans? Does this account for the differences in coverage ultimately received by whites and African Americans?

THE MEDIA REPEAT OR THE MEDIA CREATE?

Many argue that the media are thoroughly, in fact, often obsessively, committed to objectivity in reporting (e.g., Patterson 1994). Further, some claim that the primary method by which the media attempt to fulfill their objectivity standard is by reporting the range of what politicians do and say, not what those in the media themselves think (Bennett 1990; Zaller and Chiu 1996). As such, a racial emphasis in reporters' coverage need not reflect any bias on their part but merely the reality of what the candidates are doing and saying. In the media's defense, suggesting that African American politicians are committed to issues involving race is merely stating the obvious. For example, one group of researchers (Cameron, Epstein, and O'Halloran 1996) compared voting records on civil rights issues and found the *median* civil rights support score among African American Democrats in the Congress was 100%.

Skeptics of this perspective, however, note the media's general willingness to be influenced by stereotypes in political coverage. Because of the vast size of the body and the great diversity of issues that come up, those who cover Congress need to develop a stable of spokespersons to rely on, depending on the events of the day (Cook 1989; Miller 1977). The complexity of the media's task thus necessitates categorizing members; categorizing members encourages the media to label some as, for example, concerned about agriculture, some about taxes, and some about racial issues. In the process, members predominantly receive coverage only on "their" issue and can come to be stereotyped as knowing or caring only about that issue. Further entrenching this process is the cycle of information on Congress, which often begins in the specialty congressional publications (such as *Roll Call*), then appears in the national papers of note (*New York Times, Washington Post*), and then filters down to other outlets (Cook 1989). Thus, as reporters pay attention to each other's work for story ideas and information, they are exposed to each other's stereotypes.

Ultimately, despite the variety of issues they may care about and the variety of issues they may be working on, many members have trouble drawing coverage outside the areas they are known for (Cook 1989).

Critics of the media's race-centered coverage of African American leaders can rightly note that while African American members of Congress do, indeed, have dependable records on civil rights, so to do northern white Democrats (Cameron, Epstein, O'Halloran 1996). Yet, the African American member is turned to for a comment on civil rights, and the white member is turned to for issues of concern to liberals more generally.

OVERVIEW OF METHODS

To address what role African American legislators themselves have in creating an imbalance in coverage, this chapter explores the media relations efforts made by African American members of Congress, including the images they try to cultivate and their view of the process. To do so, two significant sources of information are tapped.

First, interviews with congressional press secretaries were conducted in which the priorities, goals, and experiences of the members' media efforts were described. Congressional press secretaries are the ideal source for such information, according to Cook's (1989) research, which finds that press secretaries are the media arm of House offices. Press secretaries are where media strategy comes from and where media strategy is carried out. In fact, more so than the members themselves, press secretaries have media expertise and experience and deal with the day-to-day effort to gain positive attention (Miller 1976).

In addition to asking press secretaries about the media goals of their representative, the Internet Web sites of members were scrutinized. The value of the Web sites as a source of information is that the sites represent a forum of communication in complete control of the congressional office. Members' Web sites can mention as many or as few issues as they want and present the members in any terms desired. In addition to information prepared expressly for Web visitors, congressional Web sites typically also include other communication efforts, such as the full text of members' press releases.

Thus, the press secretaries of all African American members were asked to participate, and the Web sites of African American members were analyzed. To draw conclusions about African American members' media goals relative to other members, the two comparison samples described in Chapter 2 were also utilized here. That is, one liberal control group of 20 white male members of Congress whose ideology and tenure in office are similar to those of the African American legislators was included, as was an overall control group comprising 20 white male members of Congress who are roughly representative of whites in Congress. The control groups again allow us to explore whether the images sought by African American members are unique or common to the range of liberal legislators or the range of all legislators.

PRESS SECRETARY INTERVIEWS

Interviews were obtained by calling each representative's office and asking to speak with the press secretary.[1] Respondents were informed that their office had been selected to take part in a research project on "media coverage of Congress"; they were not made aware of either the reason their office had been chosen or any of our specific hypotheses.[2] Respondents were assured that answers would not be directly attributed to them or their respective offices.

All interviews were conducted by the authors between late June and August 1998. While many press secretaries were receptive to our request, several declined to be interviewed. By far the most common explanation for refusing to participate was a standing office policy against responding to surveys of any kind. Others rejected our request on the grounds that they were serving as "acting" press secretary or simply felt they had too little experience to be of assistance. Some interviews could not be completed because of time constraints and schedule conflicts or simply because the press secretary could not be reached. In such cases, press secretaries were sent a letter requesting a written response to the interview questions. We received a total of 13 written responses, which were assimilated into the pool of 39 completed telephone interviews. Overall, our sample contains responses from 24 press secretaries working for African American members and 28 working for white members (13 in the liberal control group, and 15 from the overall control group).

The interview questionnaire contained several items designed to tap the general level of satisfaction with media coverage and allow respondents to express their feelings about the prominence of racial stereotypes in news reporting. Press secretaries were asked whether the member had been treated fairly by the media; whether the member's coverage accurately reflected his or her priorities and accomplishments; what specific disappointments they had encountered with media coverage; whether the member was subject to any media stereotypes; and, in the case of African Americans, whether there was a tendency for the media to view the member as an *African American* representative (as opposed to simply a representative).

Overall, the interviews provide strong support for the contention that the media define African American members of Congress by their race and that African American members consider this a significant problem of the media's making.

Compared with both control groups, press secretaries working for African American members were considerably more likely to complain about unfair coverage. Whereas almost every respondent in both white control groups (85% of the liberal control group; 93% of the overall control group) stated that the media generally treat them fairly, only 17%

of the press secretaries for African American members offered such positive evaluations of their media treatment. Similar results were obtained with respect to whether coverage reflected members' priorities and accomplishments (33% of the African American offices were satisfied that their coverage corresponded to their priorities and accomplishments, compared with 77% of the liberal control group and 93% of the overall control group).

Moreover, when asked about specific disappointments with media coverage, there was a tendency for press secretaries to whites and press secretaries to African Americans to emphasize different concerns. For the most part, whites' complaints usually involved a particular story or issue. For example, one press secretary felt that his boss was not getting enough credit for his efforts on issues such as child care and economic assistance. Another complained that the media had not paid enough attention to a particular bill that the member had been instrumental in getting through the House. One press secretary was livid that the media had chosen to focus only on aspects of his boss' education proposal (specifically its beneficial effect on private schools) and ignored much of what he thought the bill's true importance was. Another bemoaned a specific newspaper's inability to understand the intricacies of foreign policy.

By contrast, press secretaries to African Americans were more likely to cite a general lack of press interest in their members' leadership as their greatest disappointment. A number of press secretaries opined that their bosses were not always "taken seriously" by the media: said one, "Sometimes the media tends to focus on his community outreach efforts (walks through the district, town meetings, ribbon cuttings), but occasionally forgets his accomplishments as a lawmaker." Another noted that the media often ignored the member's contributions at congressional hearings — even when he was the most prominent member in attendance.

By far the most striking differences between African Americans and whites, however, emerged in response to the question about stereotypes. When asked if the representative had been subject to any media stereotypes, without exception press secretaries in African American offices agreed that they had. The majority quickly complained specifically about categorizations having to do with race.[3] One respondent felt that a newsmagazine had subtly stereotyped her boss by reporting that he might one day head the Congressional Black Caucus. "Why not Speaker of the House?" she wondered. Most, however, did not find much subtlety in racial stereotypes:

Definitely. Definitely. . . . Anything seen as important to the African American community has to be "validated" by an African American member. You're looked at to give the black take on things.

Any black member will be stereotyped in certain ways. [The media act as if] all black people believe and think the same things.

Definitely. The media put people into boxes.... Being black... they stereotype him as a black.

It's a conservative, white, media elite, and all they can see when they look at this office is black, black, black.

In stark contrast, press secretaries to white members were often hard-pressed to think of stereotypes that applied to them. Indeed, some seemed confused by the meaning of the question and had to ask for clarification, and many paused to think before answering. (This was not at all the case for press secretaries to American Americans, who tended to respond without any hesitation whatsoever.) Some (38% of the liberal control group; 53% of the overall control group) stated flatly that their office had not been subject to *any* media stereotypes. Of those who did mention a stereotype, virtually all complained about either a political characterization ("liberal," "right wing," "Clinton supporter," "Gingrich Clone," "Washington bureaucrat," "out of touch," etc.) or an unflattering personality trait ("hot-tempered," "confrontational," "nerdy," etc.). In *not one* case did a press secretary from a white office complain about racial or ethnic stereotyping (or anything even remotely close). By contrast, *only one* press secretary working for an African American member mentioned a stereotype that was *not* race-related ("not being accessible to the media").

It should be reemphasized that, to this point in the interview, respondents had been given no indication of our research's true purpose (i.e., there had been no direct or indirect references to race). Thus, it is all the more striking that the vast majority of press secretaries to African Americans interpreted the stereotype question as a question about race — *to the exclusion of all other potential political and personal stereotypes.* In contrast to the majority of whites, not a single press secretary for an African American member expressed any concern about being portrayed as an ideologue, a big spender, a politician, "being out of touch," or anything else commonly associated with congressional stereotypes.

Moreover, when asked directly whether there is a tendency for reporters to view and report on the member as an *African American* representative, their press secretaries universally agreed that there is.[4] Indeed, we received several strong reactions to this line of inquiry:

A reporter last week asked the Congressman, "You represent African Americans, how do they feel about the President, about the scandal?" And the Congressman said, "I represent 600,000 people, hundreds of thousands of people who don't happen to be African American, people from all walks of life, from all backgrounds."

The lowest common denominators are race and sex.... [The member] is an interloper into a previously all-white club according to some reporters.

The articles don't usually refer to his ethnicity, but I get comments from reporters: "wow, your boss is very articulate."

Never can a story be written that they don't mention he is the first black to...

It's getting better, but they're still trying to make him fit the mold.

African American. Exactly.

In addition to inquiring about how they were covered, we asked press secretaries to elaborate on how they hoped to be covered, that is, what message their office was attempting to convey. We asked, for example, what type of image they were trying to create, what types of stories they generally found most satisfying, and what an "ideal" story might look like. We also asked whether they preferred to be portrayed as "important in Washington" or "caring about the district" and the extent to which they preferred national versus local media exposure. Finally, we asked whether specific constituent groups were being targeted for media messages.

Here, the responses from African American offices were virtually indistinguishable from those of whites. Naturally, we encountered a number of personal idiosyncrasies on both the "image" and "story" items, but the same general themes emerged from both groups. Press secretaries to both African Americans and to whites wanted their bosses to be seen as "intelligent," "hardworking," "respected," "diligent," "in touch with the people," and so on, and, of course, both camps coveted stories in which the member was seen as "getting things done," "helping the district," "solving problems," "an effective legislator," "consensus builder," and so on. Given our specific interests, however, what is most noteworthy about these answers is the degree to which press secretaries to African Americans did *not* talk about an image centered on serving the interests of minority communities. By far the most commonly mentioned issues were education and job creation (79% mentioned at least one). Other answers focused on topics such as technology, infrastructure, military strength, free trade, foreign aid, crime and drugs, and agricultural assistance. Indeed, only one press secretary to an African American member specifically mentioned favorable coverage on "helping minorities." (Even here, the respondent had earlier made a point of saying her office did *not* emphasize the member's race in his public image.)

Interestingly, despite media coverage often suggesting African Americans are outsiders to the workings of Washington, press secretaries to African Americans professed slightly more interest in generating Washington-centered stories than did press secretaries in either control group. Specifically, when asked to choose between the two, 25% of the press secretaries to African Americans said their boss preferred being seen as politically important in Washington over being seen as caring about the district, while only 8% of the liberal control group and 7% of the overall control group chose that option. Similarly, when asked about the value they placed on national coverage versus local coverage, press secretaries to African Americans gave slightly greater weight to national coverage than did members of either control group (17% in the African American group preferred national coverage, compared to 15% of the liberal control group and 13% of the overall control group).[5]

When asked if they were trying to reach specific constituent groups with their media efforts, press secretaries to African Americans were more likely than whites to mention minority groups. Forty-six percent of the press secretaries to African American members made at least one reference to "ethnic groups" or "minorities," compared to only 22% in the liberal control group and none in the overall control group. However, what is again most noteworthy about the African American responses is the extent to which they did *not* focus on racial groups (and, in particular, African Americans). By far the most common reaction to this question was that the target group depended on the issue at hand. Indeed, respondents mentioned a wide array of groups that had been targeted from time to time (farmers, veterans, senior citizens, young people, whites, Jews, business owners, Hispanics, Asians, urban dwellers, teachers, students, etc.). Thus, while there was a clear tendency to highlight traditionally liberal Democratic social groups, there were very few direct references to the African American community. In fact, only one press secretary specifically listed African Americans as a frequent target group.

At the conclusion of the interviews, press secretaries were asked if they had any advice that would improve the overall content of congressional media coverage. To the extent that press secretaries for white members here offered larger criticisms of the media, they reflect no supposition of the existence of hostility or prejudice on the part of the press. Instead, these press secretaries see less than ideal or inconvenient traits of the media. For example, a number of press secretaries to white members issued calls for a harder working press corps:

I think we need to get rid of the pack journalism mentality. Where we run into the biggest problems is when one journalist parrots information from another. They take what someone else is reporting, and run with it, mistakes be damned. Rather than asking the questions themselves, rather than just doing the logic, "Does this seem plausible." As a former journalist, it is fundamental: Accuracy, Accuracy, Accuracy, that's what this process has to be about. I wouldn't gripe about accurate coverage that did not reflect well on us, that did not go our way. . . . Look at *the New Republic*, *the Boston Globe*, CNN, all admitting absolute lying in recent weeks. The media is out of control, and it's nothing that reporters actually doing their jobs, showing up, asking questions, writing it down, wouldn't solve.

The media really needs to have more knowledge of the issues before they start working on a story. The reporters who I deal with waste too much of my time, and too much of my boss's time asking about background details on an issue, instead of asking what they should be asking . . . questions that only a Congressional office could answer, such as what is happening in the Congress, what my boss is doing on the issue, why he's doing it. It shows real laziness on the part of the reporter when they come here as a first step.

I am personally amazed at how little reporters understand how Congress works. Because of their lack of knowledge, they really miss out on the impact these federal laws will have on localities. I can count on one hand the number of seasoned professionals that are out there who really understand the in's and out's of Congress and comprehend the reality of issues.

I'd like to convince editors, producers, and reporters to do their homework. Often their knowledge of government and Congressional procedure is very shallow — which results in very shallow coverage. The biggest problem with media isn't bias, it's ignorance.

Quite strikingly, press secretaries to African American members asked instead for "openness," "fairness," "a chance to show who we are before the media makes up its mind." One press secretary commented,

What we desperately need is for editors and reporters to stop creating the story before they've written it — to stop writing the story before they interview the member. Because what they do is write up the story first, then call us for a quote, and then they just insert his two sentences at the pre-planned breaks. They make us fit into their pre-conceived notions, their stereotypes.

Taken in conjunction, our press secretary interviews and content analysis from Chapter 2 provide a very clear picture. Simply put, African Americans in Congress are not subject to the same media treatment as whites. They are more likely to be stereotyped according to race, featured in stories on race and racial issues, and dissatisfied with their overall media coverage.

Do African American members sell themselves this way? Do they emphasize racial issues above all else and encourage the media to pigeonhole them in that role? The press secretaries' perspective is that they do not — that their goals are to present a more diversified image, and that their communication efforts are consistent with that.

In an effort to observe congressional communication independently of what the press secretaries say it is, we turn to the Internet Web sites for members of Congress. Web sites provide access to vast quantities of congressional communication, including information geared specifically for the voters and information targeted for the media, providing a third party the chance to see if African American members are in any way supporting the media's race-centered view of their work.

IMAGES ON THE WEB

While the Web is undoubtedly a developing medium for congressional offices, its significance as an outlet for members' communication goals should not be ignored. Representative Edolphus Towns (D-NY) refers to his Web site as "a vehicle of empowerment for all."[6] Charles Rangel (D-NY), in his welcome message on his Web site, explains, "I have established this Web page with the needs of my constituents in mind. It will provide faster access to information on my activities in the U.S. House of Representatives and in my Congressional

District. . . . I encourage you to use this site as yet another way to let your voices be heard."[7]

Moreover, 97% of House offices have Web sites[8]; House Web sites receive as many as 1,000 visits per month[9]; and Web sites tend to feature substantially similar content as the traditional congressional newsletters that are sent to all constituents.[10] By 1998 the expectation that representatives would have Web and e-mail systems up and running was strong enough that some newspapers featured stories on members who did not have computer communication systems. The *Seattle Times* quoted one voter as asking the paper to do a story on those members of Congress "who don't bother to get with the times and get e-mail."[11] Finally, Web sites are considered significant enough that, just as franking privileges are suspended during the two months preceding an election, House members are not allowed to update their Web sites during the two months prior to an election.

Each Web site of members in the sample (30 African American members have Web sites, 16 members in the liberal control group, and 18 in the overall control group) was explored to determine what issues the members presented as priorities, what legislative accomplishments the members highlighted, what groups the members aligned themselves with, and how the members presented their experience in Washington.

All member Web sites have a biography page that presents the representatives' background information and, to varying degrees, their political agenda. Virtually all the Web sites complement the biography with a separate page discussing the member's issue agenda (which vary from including as few as 1 issue to as many as 30), and most offer recent press releases in their sites. Finally, a number of members highlight an issue or two with special links and separate pages dedicated just to that issue. Typically, in addition to member-created material, sites offer a number of nonpolitical links, such as to the representative's home area, and a number of links to political, but not member-specific, information such as the congressional calendar, the Library of Congress, and the congressional legislative bill tracking service.

Between June and October 1998, all member-created material within each site was read, and all mentions of issues (and the amount of space dedicated to each issue), membership in groups, mentions of Washington accomplishments, and presentations of the members' legislative experiences were recorded by two coders who were unaware of the previously described findings.

Racial Issues/Civil Rights Emphasis

Criticizing the media for portraying African American members as primarily interested in questions of race and civil rights is not evidence of stereotyping, of course, if it is an accurate depiction of what members do and say. In fact, this characterization is not without some basis in reality. The vast majority of African American members highlight their civil rights and racial issues record on the Web, while these matters almost go unmentioned among members of the control groups (Table 3.1). Moreover, most African American members mention their affiliation with an African American or civil rights organization (most frequently the Congressional Black Caucus, but many list the National Association for the Advancement of Colored People [NAACP] and other civil rights groups), while only one member of the control groups mentions an affiliation with such a group (90% of African Americans mention a race/civil rights group affiliation, 6% of the liberal control group do so, and the number is zero in the overall control group).

With that said, civil rights and racial concerns are only part — for most African American members, a small part — of what they say they do. As such, African American legislators as a group display interest in a host of issues that have no direct bearing on civil rights or racial concerns. As shown in Table 3.1, education, human rights, and poverty policy are all areas that African American legislators give far more attention to than does either of the control groups.

Moreover, most African American members do not feature civil rights or racial issues as the most prominent issue area on their Web page. In fact, 60% of African American legislators dedicate more space to at least one other issue, and all African American legislators dedicate most of their total space to issues other than civil rights and racial concerns.

Perhaps even more significantly, when it comes to listing their accomplishments in office, only 13% of African American legislators feature civil rights or racial issues as an area in which they have had their biggest legislative accomplishment. In fact, the most frequently occurring area highlighted by African American legislators as their highest achievement in Congress was bringing home dollars for economic development (Table 3.2). Fighting crime and assuming an important role in party leadership were tied for the second most mentioned accomplishment. Such a pattern surely does not bespeak an exclusive focus on race relations and civil rights that some in the media

Table 3.1
Issues Highlighted on Web Sites

	African American	Liberal Control	Overall Control
Civil Rights/ Racial Issues	77%	6%	0%
Education	70%	56%	44%
Human Rights	47%	25%	6%
Poverty	97%	75%	33%

N=64.
Source: House members' Web sites.

Table 3.2
Most Cited Accomplishments of House Members

African American	Liberal Control	Overall Control
Economic Development (47%)	Poverty Legislation (25%)	Taxes/Budget (33%)
Crime (26%)	Transportation (25%)	Economic Development (28%)
Party Leadership (26%)	Party Leadership (25%)	Transportation (22%)

N=64.
Source: House members' Web sites.

perceive. Far from placing them in any extreme, their focus on economic development is not at all unique — as the members of the overall control group also highlight economic development as one of their biggest areas of achievement.

Of course, even as members emphasize the same achievements, the press response to those accomplishments varies tremendously. Representative Corrine Brown (D-FL) explains, "When a white Congressman encourages business development in his district, reporters say he's doing his job; when I bring potential investors to the district, my hometown paper questions my involvement. They think I should stick to issues like welfare."[12]

It is, nevertheless, possible that African American legislators have understated their racial issues and civil rights commitment and that the media's focus on racial issues and civil rights reflects the reality of their political agenda, if not the image the members have sought. To investigate this possibility, the legislation introduced by each member of the sample during the 105th session of Congress was categorized by topic. Replicating the findings of the Web site analysis, most African American legislators were active in civil rights (63% introduced civil rights/racial issue legislation, approximately one piece of legislation per African American member), but again, other issue areas, specifically, poverty-ameliorating legislation, received greater attention from African American legislators (69% introduced anti-poverty legislation, slightly more than two pieces of legislation per African American member). In total, civil rights and racial issue proposals made up less than 10% of the legislation introduced by African American members of Congress.

Parochial Outsiders

In addition to not communicating a message that all they care about are racial issues, the prominently touted accomplishment of achieving party leadership (which appears more frequently in African American members' sites than in the overall control group and about as frequently as in the liberal control group) hardly implies that African American members are responsible for their portrayal as legislative outsiders. Even more telling, just as in the two control groups, African American legislators are most likely to describe their Washington experience as one in which they have been "leaders" or "leading the way" in their congressional work (Table 3.3). In fact, their three most frequent assessments of their legislative experience are the same as the top three descriptions used by the overall control group. Again, African American legislators are not suggesting they are shut out of the congressional process but rather that they are just as likely to present themselves as integral to the process.

Even the suggestion in the media that African American members' concerns are more grounded in their districts goes unsupported in the members' sites, as African American members are slightly more likely (33%) to mention a foreign policy concern than either control group (31% of the liberal group, 22% of the overall control group).

Ultimately, the Web sites of African American members of Congress suggest very little in the way of an exclusive focus on race, an abnormal parochial concern with the district, or an inability to meaningfully participate in the legislative process. Thus, it would appear, as the press secretaries to African American members suggested, that these are conclusions born in the media, not with these members.

Table 3.3
Most Used Description of Legislative Experience

African American	Liberal Control	Overall Control
Leader/Leading (47%)	Leader/Leading (44%)	Leader/Leading (33%)
Fought For/Fighting (20%)	Fought For/Fighting (19%)	Fought For/Fighting (22%)
Best/Most Effective (17%)	Created Landmark Legislation (19%)	Best/Most Effective (22%)

N=64.
Source: House members' Web sites.

SUMMARY AND CONCLUSION

The media's racially centered view of African American legislators is a subject of great concern to African American legislators and their press staff. Compared with those in our control groups who work for white members of Congress, the press secretaries to African American members are less likely to believe their member is treated fairly, less likely to believe that their member's priorities and accomplishments are covered adequately, and more likely to believe that there is a general problem in media coverage. Moreover, they universally believe that their member is subject to being viewed by the media as an African American representative, rather than a representative who happens to be African American.

Neither the responses of these press secretaries nor an analysis of congressional Web sites can account for this pattern; that is, the media's depiction of African American representatives as being narrowly focused on race and operating outside the wheels of power does not originate with the members themselves. Rather, members' Web sites reveal that the picture they paint of themselves includes a much greater diversity of issue commitments, a significant focus on accomplishments that have nothing directly to do with racial issues, and a portrayal that gives African Americans in Congress equal standing with white members in terms of their influence in the legislative process.

None of this is meant to imply that African American legislators are less than committed to civil rights and racial issues. Instead, seeing African American legislators as if racial issues define them to the exclusion of all other beliefs and concerns is, as one press secretary put it, "like saying a city is just its main street, or a university is just its best known department. You miss most of what is going on if you define someone, or anything, like that." As critic Christopher Campbell argues, "Despite journalism's trumpeted efforts as democracy's champion, when it comes to race the watchdog is snoozing comfortably in its doghouse" (1995, 136).

In contrast to the media's perspective, African American members often go to tremendous lengths to see beyond race, even in situations in which racial issues have almost blinding intensity. To wit, Representative John Lewis, allowed to communicate in his own voice, without the distortion of reporters, wrote an eloquent op-ed article on the death of George Wallace. Wallace, the former segregationist governor of Alabama, once vowed never to be "outniggered" in an election.[13] Lewis did not write to condemn George Wallace and his race-baiting. Instead, Lewis argued, "George Wallace should be remembered for his capacity to change. And we are better as a nation because of our capacity to forgive and to acknowledge that our political leaders are human and largely a reflection of the social currents in the river of history." Lewis proclaimed, "Through genuine repentance and forgiveness the soul of our nation is redeemed."[14] Ironically, for most African American members, the discussion of race is about a commitment to inclusion, while in the media it is conveyed as a preference for exclusion.

Moreover, the examples of African American members' diverse commitment to the dispossessed are so great as to be nearly indescribable. One poignant example from the Web sites stands out. Some of the most passionate voices for women's rights and well-being emanate from the Congressional Black Caucus, including male members of the caucus.[15] Representative Major Owens' (D-NY) Web site[16] features poetry and rap songs the member has penned, including this recent condemnation of men and celebration of women:

> Let the mothers lead the fight
> Sisters snatch the future from the night
> Dangerous dumb males have made a mess on the right...
> Human history is a long ugly tale
> Tragedy guided by the frail monster male...
> Across time hear our loud terrified wail
> Holocaust happens when silly males fail...

Ultimately, it is not inaccurate to suggest a racial focus on the part of African Americans in Congress, but it is very misleading. African American leaders' image in the media — that they care about African Americans first, last, and always — does not leave sufficient room to say that these legislators' concern is for those in need. As Payne (1988) argues, the danger of media that offer false representations is that the media's perceptions can become the voters' reality.

Instead of media distortion, what African American legislators want is a chance to speak for themselves and present the true nature of their concerns. As one press secretary put it,

The press looks at this office and sees black; we care about blacks; we think about blacks. What they don't see, can't see, or won't see is that this office is not about blacks or whites. It's about a socially conscious approach to government. It's about being unafraid to be a crusader for those who need. We represent the least...the last...the lost.

NOTES

1. While position titles vary slightly from office to office, our calls were invariably directed to individuals whose primary duties involved regular contact with the media. Each subject was asked to provide a brief description of his or her position, and in all cases respondents offered some variant of "press relations" as his or her principal role. A few respondents' duties also included tasks such as legislative assistance, speechwriting, "Web master," etc., but in every instance it was clear that the individual considered himself or herself the office's primary media contact.

2. When pressed for more information regarding the nature of the study, we offered only that our research was looking into issues such as "accuracy in media coverage of Congress." If asked how the member's office came to be included in the sample, we revealed only that our sample had been designed to include members with certain demographic and political backgrounds and that this office happened to meet our criteria. In short, every effort was made to assure that our specific interests were not revealed, that is, that race would not be artificially injected into a respondent's thoughts.

3. One press secretary talked indirectly about racial stereotyping even before she had been asked the question. When queried about specific disappointments with the member's coverage, she complained about receiving calls from reporters whenever a "black issue" was in the news. "Whenever there's an affirmative action vote, [the media] call to get [his] point of view."

4. One respondent initially claimed that the member was generally not portrayed in this light but later mentioned that race had indeed been emphasized in some of their most recent campaign coverage. Every other press secretary agreed at the outset that at least some reporters tend to think of (and report on) their boss as an "African American representative."

5. See Dewhirst (1983) for discussion of the local focus of most congressional press offices.

6. Towns' site is (www.house.gov/towns/). His welcome message appears at (www.house.gov/towns/welcome_message.html).

7. Rangel's site is (www.house.gov/rangel/). His welcome message appears at (www.house.gov/rangel/welcmsg.htm).

8. As of September 25, 1999. At the time of our Web site analysis, this figure was 90%.

9. Most House Web sites do not feature a counter noting how many visits the site has received. Among those that do, Patrick Kennedy's (D-RI) site reported receiving 25,000 visits in just over two years (www.house.gov/patrickkennedy/),

and Bob Goodlatte's (R-VA) site counted over 7,000 visitors in its seven months on-line (www.house.gov/goodlatte/).

10. For example, see Jerold Nadler's (D-NY) Web site (www.house.gov/nadler/), which features a complete copy of his latest newsletter. The issues and Nadler's role in them are quite consistent in the newsletter and on the Web site.

11. *Seattle Times*, December 17, 1998.

12. Correspondence with the authors, November 5, 1999.

13. See Frady 1968, 127.

14. *New York Times*, September 16, 1998.

15. Specific legislative proposals most frequently dealt with domestic violence and with women's health care.

16. Owens' site is (www.house.gov/owens/).

4

"It's True, Isn't It?" The View from the Newsroom

Albert Wynn (D-MD) and James Moran Jr. (D-VA) are liberal Democratic members of the House of Representatives, both from the Washington, D.C. area.[1] Despite their similarities, media coverage of the two representatives is quite distinct — a distinction that seems to flow from one difference between the two: Wynn is African American, and Moran is white.

In a previous study (Zilber and Niven 1996) we examined all stories in national newspapers from 1993 to 1996 that profiled either member. The juxtaposition of Wynn and Moran coverage offers a striking case in which race (both the representatives' race and the racial makeup of their districts) underlies the reporting.

First, it is noteworthy that every Wynn article contains at least one reference to his race, and four in five articles mention the racial makeup of his district. One *Washington Post* story begins: "When Albert R. Wynn was elected to represent Maryland's 4th Congressional District two years ago, he instantly made history, becoming the first member of Congress to be elected from a majority-black suburban district."[2] By contrast, none of the articles on Moran contain even a single reference to his race or the racial makeup of his district.

The differences in coverage extend well beyond mere allusions to race, however. In fact, it would not be an overstatement to say that race and race-related issues are at the core of every article in which Wynn is mentioned. One article discusses Wynn's views on the Million Man March and Louis Farrakhan; another focuses on his constituents' views on affirmative action; and so on. In fact, only one article contains any significant discussion of Wynn's congressional activities that was not in some way linked to race. Somewhat ironically, the major thrust of that story is that Wynn's Washington activities had received very little attention.[3]

Again, the contrast in coverage could hardly be more pronounced: not one of the Moran articles contains even a passing reference to race or issues directly related to race. Typical of Moran's coverage are stories revolving around issues such as health care, education, childhood disease research, Bosnia, or benefits for federal employees.

Consistent with the data presented in Chapter 2, Representative Moran is much more likely to be described as a "player" in the Washington power struggle or placed within the context of Congress as an institution. Several articles, for example, refer to Moran's opposition to the president's health care plan and efforts to "reinvent" the federal government. Others focus on Moran's battles to pass his own legislative initiatives. In the most glaring case, the *Washington Post* portrays Moran as a staunch defender of his institution: "In a year when candidates of all parties are heaping scorn upon the federal government, [Moran] is a conspicuous exception. He is proud to serve in Congress, and he is quick to say so."[4] By contrast, Wynn's coverage is much more likely to focus on his relationship with his constituents or the African American community. One *Post* article begins: "One after another, speakers stepped to the lectern at a Capitol Hill forum hosted by Rep. Albert R. Wynn yesterday to proclaim the continuing need for affirmative action, denounce Republican efforts to dismantle it and criticize the media coverage of the issue. The audience, mostly from the Democrat's Prince George's County district, was firmly on board."[5] Another story leads with: "It was nominally the kickoff for Beatrice P. Tignor's campaign for Prince George's county executive, but there was little doubt that the man in charge was the burly politician known to almost everyone in the crowd simply as Albert. Clapping his hands, leading the cheers, bellowing at the top of his lungs and aiming barbs at his political rivals, Rep. Albert R. Wynn was clearly in his element."[6]

In short, the Wynn-Moran comparison seems to be a microcosm of the racialized findings of our content analysis. Wynn is portrayed as a "black representative" from a "black district" whose primary concerns are those of his constituents and other blacks. Moran is portrayed as a more "typical" representative with a wide array of policy interests — a member who is closely associated with his institution and immersed in the Washington power struggle.

The data in Chapters 2 and 3 indicate that the media portray politicians in a racialized fashion, and the politicians themselves do not appear responsible for this distinction. Why, then, would reporters emphasize race to such a degree? To understand reporters' roles in creating this coverage, as well as their perspective on it, we followed two paths. First, we used the aforementioned study of Wynn-Moran coverage as a point of departure for a discussion with ten political reporters from around the country on the role of race in covering Congress. Further, we surveyed a national sample of over 100 political reporters in an attempt to discern whether reporters' reactions to race fit psychological explanations of stereotyping.

SOURCES OF BIASED STEREOTYPES

Bias against African American politicians by the media is not portrayed in academic work as a product of hostility. Rather, scholars suggest that the tendency to define African American leaders distinctively from whites is a product of lack of thought and understanding (Campbell 1995; Payne 1988; Barber and Gandy 1990). Inordinate attention to race is the product of "an individual's cultural experience," Barber and Gandy (1990, 213) argue, an experience that "produces a tendency to notice some aspects of phenomena and ignore others; to identify some things as normal, and therefore not newsworthy, and others as unusual, thus worthy of review or comment."

Psychological research offers two quite plausible theories that suggest why individuals might approach race with heightened attention but little thought or understanding. Both theories, the out-group effect and the distribution effect, see difference as a source of bias.

The Out-group Effect

In the out-group effect, *the difference between the perceiver and the target* is the source of biased perceptions. People categorize and divide the world into in-groups, which are people in the same category as themselves, and out-groups, which are people outside their category.

Categories run the gamut of identifiable traits, but for many, race is a most prominent factor.

The significance of this categorization process is that categories often feed our initial perceptions about people, especially for members of the out-group. For example, the lack of similarity between the in-group perceiver and the out-group target can feed an out-group homogeneity assumption. This assumption leads perceivers to pay greater attention to the differences between out-group members and in-group members and encourages perceivers to lump out-group members together, casting all out-group members with the same qualities. (On the out-group effect, see, e.g., Jones, Wood, and Quattrone 1981; Judd and Park 1988; Mackie and Worth 1989; Carpenter 1993.)

In addition to homogenizing the out-group, perceivers tend to arrive at different explanations for in-group and out-group behaviors and outcomes. Most importantly, while the in-group is assumed to be responsible for its own successes, the success of out-group members is often written off as the product of luck or special circumstances and therefore reflecting no real accomplishment (Lau and Russell 1980). As such, the in-group is viewed not just more distinctively but more positively than out-group members.

For African American representatives, the potential danger of the out-group effect is reflected in the overwhelmingly white reporting corps. Because African American representatives do not share surface similarities with white reporters, these reporters may define African Americans as part of their out-group and therefore be less sensitive to distinctions between African American members. If that were to occur, it would not be the individual characteristics of the African American member that would shape reporters' perceptions and their subsequent coverage. Instead, reporters' perceptions of the entire out-group would inform their perceptions and color their coverage.

As such, coverage would not reflect the individual issue interests of *an African American member* as much as the reporters' perceptions of what *African Americans* are interested in. Coverage of civil rights could be particularly affected by the out-group effect, as researchers suggest that perceivers pay particular attention to group status when there is even the slightest prompt to think about the existence of the specific group (Devine 1989).

White representatives, conversely, as members of the white reporters' in-group, could benefit from the assumptions fostered by in-group status.

Those assumptions include a belief that the in-group target person is similar to the perceiver in attitudes, values, and personality (Piliavin 1987), and is more than likely highly competent (Klahr 1969).[7]

Thus, it is with potentially devastating consequences that African American representatives would be defined as members of the out-group: lumped together as thoughtlessly sharing the same traits and narrow interests as other African American members, while having little in common with those who write the news, and assumed to have less to do with their successes and more to do with their failures than white members. In sum, in-group members are inclined to positively evaluate fellow in-group members, while out-group members are consigned to their status as nonindividuals in a group defined by its differences and shortcomings.

This explanation has a surface plausibility to it given the demographic makeup of media professionals. Walter Lippman once warned that reporters should not be sent to cover stories more than seven miles from their homes; metaphorically, racial issues tend to be covered by strangers from a faraway land. Van Dijk (1991) laments that most coverage of civil rights and African American politics is written by white reporters who experience the world through their own white perspective, frequently augmented by the views of white political experts. Of note, half of all U.S. newspapers have no African American reporters (Campbell 1995), while white newsroom staff outnumber African Americans 17 to 1.[8] Despite the stated goal of the American Society of Newspaper Editors (ASNE) to increase diversity, the number of African Americans on staff at U.S. newspapers actually dropped between 1995 and 1998.[9] In fact, while in 1978 ASNE set a goal of an American newsroom that looked like America, more than four out of ten newspapers lacked a nonwhite newsroom staffer in 1998![10] One media critic argues that newspapers suffer from "diversity fatigue"; they intend to diversify, and some act on the goal, but the persistent difficulty of the task has led many news organizations to abandon the effort.[11]

Moreover, the out-group effect is implicitly blamed by many African American members of Congress for what they perceive is slanted media coverage. The Congressional Black Caucus has held hearings on the lack of diversity among reporters, and caucus members such as William Clay (D-MO) have concluded that the overrepresentation of whites in the media is the root cause of racialized coverage (1992, 244).

The Distribution Effect

A second explanation for media stereotyping focuses not on the difference between the perceiver and the target but on *the difference between the target and the typical member of the target's profession*. In other words, the distribution effect causes people to associate a profession with the attributes of those who typically serve in it, making specific demographic traits seem like virtual qualifications for the job. Thus, the paucity of African Americans in public office may encourage onlookers to form a subconscious association between political leadership and whites.

Research on the distribution effect has emphasized this process in gender discrimination, but the same principles apply to race. Regarding gender, when one encounters a female in an occupation area dominated by males, the incongruity feeds doubts concerning the appropriateness of the woman's position (Eagly, Makhijani, and Klonsky 1992). This results in abstractions of the sexes, definitions of who the sexes are and should be, based on their distribution in productive roles (Yount 1986; Kiesler 1975; Eagly and Wood 1982). For race this would mean defining jobs overwhelmingly held by whites as jobs where whites' behavior is particularly suited to the occupation. African Americans who seek or hold such a position will be compared with the more typical holder of the job, and any differences between the two will be particularly prominent to the perceiver.

Eagly and Wood (1982) emphasize that this does not mean that people judge members of the dominant distribution to be inherently superior. The danger lies, instead, in the initial assumptions people make, which without contradicting information, will result in the dominant distribution being assumed to be more qualified and successful because of the status associated with their group's hold on the profession. Meanwhile, those in the rare distribution are lumped together because of their distinct and unusual position (Eagly and Mladinic 1989).

Hoffman and Hurst (1990) argue that the distribution effect serves us as protection from having to confront the possibility of societal or personal bias. By attributing the dominance of a demographic group in a profession to its unique qualifications, we remove the possibility that its dominance is based on discrimination.

Ultimately, if the distribution effect influences reporters, those who work in areas where African American representatives are particularly rare will pay greater attention to differences between the dominant demographic group (whites) and the rare demographic group (African Americans). Affected reporters will assume that the traits of whites are both normal and associated with success and will homogenize African American politicians as a rare class of political oddities.

The obvious surface plausibility of the out-group effect is the relative paucity of African American members and African American leaders in Congress. For example, the majority of states have never sent an African American to Congress.[12] More startling, when considering all House terms served in the twentieth century, African Americans have filled less than one-third of 1% of those seats.[13] In the Senate, African Americans have served less than one-fifth of 1% of this century's terms.[14] African Americans have held a grand total of zero positions as Speaker, majority leader, or minority leader in the House and zero positions as majority leader, minority leader, or president pro tem of the Senate. There is, therefore, an obvious difference between the typical member of Congress or the typical leader of Congress and the African American members who have served.

This might also be a more plausible explanation for racialized coverage than the out-group effect because of the strong similarities between white and African American reporters. Political columnist John Leo argues that reporters, whether white or African American, "have gone to the same schools" and "think the same thoughts" and therefore should not be expected to produce racially distinctive thoughts, conclusions, or reporting.[15]

The importance of the distinction between out-group bias and distribution bias is the great difference in their future implications. Out-group bias is based on the difference between the perceiver and the target; thus, the best way to alleviate bias against African American politicians would be to create a more diverse newsroom. Distribution bias, based on the difference between most politicians and African American politicians, would suggest we need to elect more African American leaders in order to alleviate the media stereotypes they are subjected to.

WHY AREN'T REPORTERS ABOVE BIAS?

One immediate reaction to the assertion that reporters may incorporate racial stereotypes into their coverage is to assume that members of our well-educated reporting profession are in all likelihood, above stereotypes and bias.

Moreover, producers and editors believe that bias is a threat to credibility and, ultimately, that a threat to credibility is a threat to profitability (Kurtz 1994). Many in media management are so adamant about the need to produce unbiased reportage that they scrutinize not just their reporters' writing but also their private lives! Kurtz (1994) notes that media outlets ranging from the most prominent (the *New York Times*, the *Washington Post*) to the obscure (the *Fairfield Ledger*) have investigated and ultimately forbidden the political activity of reporters, activity that took place outside the office and on the reporters' own time. Editors of the *Washington Post* warned all their reporters (even those who exclusively cover nonpolitical fare such as sports) that political advocacy on their own time was "unprofessional" and that forgoing the right to political expression "is the choice we make when we choose to work in this business" (Kurtz 1994, 148).

Nevertheless, the inclination to assume that political reporters have a strong incentive to overcome perceptual bias is challenged by research that has found in-group favoritism is perpetuated even when such behavior is disadvantageous for the in-group (Brown, Collins, and Schmidt 1988; Turner, Brown, and Tajfel 1979). Beyond self-interest, many would imagine that education and expertise necessary to become a reporter would deter people from falling prey to perceptual bias. Jackman, however, has argued that education and position do not liberate people from intergroup negativism (Jackman and Muha 1984). In fact, education can bolster bias; when you believe yourself to be knowledgeable about something, you can more easily convince yourself that your decisions are based on expertise, not prejudice. Accordingly, Jussim (1990) argues that those with high belief certainty have a low accuracy motivation because when they believe they are right, they do not invest much effort in seeking objective confirmation. According to Jackman and Muha (1984), instead of lifting people beyond bias, education primarily enables people to adopt an outlook that protects their interests. When reporters are covering an African American representative, if their instincts suggest the representative is distinct from white members, the reporter could immediately assume that the conclusion is based on political knowledge and give the situation little further thought.

Gans (1980), in a study of newsroom attitudes and behaviors, stresses the enormous importance of the standing assumptions that reporters utilize. Having to constantly produce written product under deadlines encourages reporters to perceive and react, not to perceive, question their perceptions, perceive again, question those perceptions, and so on. The process of reporting necessitates the use of standing assumptions, assumptions that can then fester unchallenged by the reporter or by anyone else. Psychologists confirm that when time is limited, perceivers reduce their reliance on perceptions of individuals and increase their reliance on perceptions of groups (Burnstein and Vinokur 1975; Kruglanski 1989; Jamieson and Zanna 1989; Koller and Wicklund 1988). In other words, the less time one has and the more difficult the task one faces, the more one is apt to rely on biased categorizations, and the less one is able to counter one's initial inclinations.

Gans' (1980) research on the media explores the standing political assumptions that are popularly held by reporters, including the inherent value of democracy, of capitalism, and of the American way of life. These assumptions are not merely themes that reporters occasionally focus on; they are a means to approach their work, a perspective through which to view events. As a consequence, reporters utilize these assumptions without even realizing it, but not without the assumptions having a fundamental influence on their reporting. When you approach reporting with the assumption that capitalism must be valued, you look for waste in the federal government, and you decry it. When you approach reporting with the assumption that the American way of life is correct, you look for confirmation, such as the *New York Times* reporter who unearthed the tidbit that no two nations that have McDonald's restaurants have ever gone to war with each other. When you approach reporting Congress with the assumption that African American representatives are interested in race and little else, you ask African Americans about race, and when they answer your questions by talking about race, your unexamined assumption is further buttressed. When other reporters read your story, they see again an African American representative talking about race, furthering their own assumption that race is all African Americans in Congress are interested in.

These assumptions that Gans writes about are consistent with the process psychologists label "expectancy effects." Snyder argues, "Events in the social world may be as much effects of individuals' beliefs as they are causes of these beliefs" (1984, 294). In other words, the expectation that someone (an African American representative) will give a distinct answer will lead to different treatment by the perceiver (the reporter), which can alter the African American's answers and ultimately result in a confirmation of the original stereotype.

A press secretary to an African American member of Congress suggested just such a process:

Well instead of asking what do you think, they [reporters] ask, "Don't you think it's x, would you call it y." Well, you set me up to give an answer, then I finally give it, then basically you decided what I was going to say before I said it.

REPORTER INTERVIEWS

How do reporters see this process? How do they respond to racialized coverage? Is it fair to ask African Americans different questions, to portray African American members differently, to think of them differently? We interviewed ten reporters who have covered Congress or congressional campaigns to find out what they think or at least what their public answers are to these questions.

Subjects of the interview were found by starting with a local reporter one author had contact with. The locally based political reporter was asked to provide the name of a colleague who might be willing to be interviewed, and this procedure was followed until between March and April 1999 we had spoken to ten political reporters from across the country who agreed to a telephone interview on racialized reporting.[16] Subjects were promised that their comments would be recorded anonymously.

Responses cannot be considered representative of the population of reporters, nor can the possibility that their responses are affected by the researchers' specific area of interests be eliminated. Rather, the value of the interviews was the depth of conversation with these reporters, for which we would have no other means of access. Additionally, the interviews provided a structure for the survey that was later sent to a nationally representative sample of reporters.

REPORTERS ON RACIALIZED REPORTING

Why do reporters make such prominent racial distinctions, as they did in the Wynn and Moran coverage that opens this chapter? We began each interview by reading reporters a synopsis of the differences in coverage between these two Democrats. By far the most prominent answer as to why reporters make such prominent racial distinctions is that they make them because they are "true."

Reporter A: It's true, isn't it? Everything you just described to me is true. Wynn does advocate affirmative action, and Moran is active on health care.

Reporter B: We take enough heat for allegations that we are unfair — but what you just said is that articles on Wynn focus on who Wynn is, and articles on Moran focus on who Moran is. You are complaining about articles because they cite true things about Wynn and true things about Moran.

Reporter H: Is there anything factually incorrect in either story? This is just run of the mill kind of information here.

Question: Are you concerned that something can be true without being accurate? It would be true, for example, to describe both the *Washington Post* and *Brick Town News* as newspapers, but it would hardly convey the accurate information that one is a world leader, and the other a tiny local paper that is given away.

Reporter B: Do you honestly think it makes no difference that a member is Black? You don't really think every white and every Black member of the House wake up in the morning thinking about the same issues and the same concerns. I would say it is both true and accurate that Black members have significantly different concerns than white members.

Reporter G: Of course that is a concern. Everything we do is to present a simplification of the whole. We couldn't otherwise do our job without relying in part on information that is true but not completely accurate. But in this case, who is it that you think is being hurt? Who is it that is supposed to be the victim of this inaccuracy? Do you think Albert Wynn wants coverage that says he's nearly indistinguishable from the white members of the House? Of course not, he benefits from this coverage . . . . How do you think reporters get those ideas but from the members themselves? It strikes me that you are criticizing the media for giving African American politicians the kind of coverage they ask for.

Question: Does the media have any obligation to portray these members more broadly rather than caricaturing them?

Reporter B: Would you ask that if we portrayed a senior Republican as worrying endlessly about the capital gains tax? We obviously have no obligation to make them into more than what they are.

Question: Is there any reason for concern?

Reporter I: Generally speaking, what we do could always be better. In that sense, there is always reason for concern. I would say that, though, about any political coverage, any Congressional coverage, not just about coverage of Blacks and whites.

Question: Did you know no African American member of Congress has ever gone on to win statewide office?

Reporter B: I guess that's right. You don't mean to tell me that that's my fault. My goodness, we get blamed for everything.

Reporter A: That has a lot to do with African Americans not choosing to run — look at how many successful Blacks in the House who have stayed there because they have had power there.

We were struck by how reluctant these reporters are to see racialized coverage as a problem or as a product of the media's assumptions and perspectives. Nevertheless, there is perhaps something even more notable about the preceding series of comments. They all come from African American reporters! While we tend to think of stereotypes as originating in an "us versus them" lack of familiarity, the African American reporters we interviewed were uniformly unwilling to sympathize with African American politicians. Our conversations with white reporters yielded much the same perspective — racialized coverage is true, unproblematic, and not caused by reporters.

This suggests that stereotyping of African American politicians is not a matter of the out-group effect — the surface difference between white reporters and African American politicians. To test whether this conclusion holds for a random sample of reporters and in a setting where respondents are not sensitized to our interest in race, in April 1999 we sent surveys to 200 Washington-based newspaper reporters who were randomly selected from among the thousands who hold press credentials to cover Congress.[17] After a total of three mailings of a cover letter and survey, we received 107 usable responses. While a response rate in the vicinity of 50% is typical for a survey of elites, our confidence in the representativeness of our respondents is buttressed by the close relationship between the characteristics of the respondents and the characteristics of the overall population. Among the variables we have access to for both groups (gender, region, circulation size of the newspaper), the respondents do not have any statistically significant differences.[18]

To ensure the diversity in our respondents necessary to fully analyze the data, we also identified 30 African American reporters on the credentials list.[19] We added those reporters to our sample and wrote to them up to five times. Twenty of the 30 ultimately responded, giving us a total of 127 respondents.

Reporters were told that this was a study of the political perceptions of the media, with the goal of assessing whether there was partisan bias in the media. To buttress our claim, we included a brief overview of research comparing coverage of Democratic and Republican governors (Niven 1999) and explained to the reporters that we wanted to explore their perceptions on this matter with regard to Congress. There was no mention of the racial focus of the study. Reporters were assured that their responses would be recorded anonymously and were offered a token reward in the form of a small donation to charity made for each survey returned. (The mailing is described in detail in the Appendix).

THE STATE OF THE MEDIA

When we asked reporters to assess the state of the media as it pertains to covering Congress, as shown in Table 4.1, reporters gave their trade an average grade of B- for its work.[20]

Space was provided for reporters to comment on their criticisms of the congressional coverage, and the most frequently cited concerns basically dealt with "easy" coverage and "cheap" coverage. Reporters feel that too many in their profession write the easiest stories about the easiest topics.

I think it is at some level inevitable, which does not make it right, that we'll be more likely to cover things that are easy to cover. When we let ourselves be led around by members, then we can really miss the story, and wind up serving their purpose more than serving our readers.

When you need to get out a story now, you can't get every source you would like, follow every trail you want to. Sometimes you are happy to get out what passed, by how much, and who's claiming victory. Subterfuge and subtext are left for the book writers.

Too much of what goes out is sloppy, too many errors get out. My absolute favorite example was a story about the number of errors in the media, and the fact that ASNE was so upset about it that they were going to spend a billion dollars to

Table 4.1
Reporters Grade Congressional Coverage

A	19%
B	39%
C	33%
D	8%
F	1%
Average	B-

N = 127.
Source: Authors' survey of congressional reporters.

study the problem. The next day a correction appeared in the paper noting that the report had overstated ASNE's budget by a mere 999 million dollars.

Apart from the ease and reliability of coverage, reporters are concerned with the topics, tone, and style of what they report. They fear that commercial concerns encourage too many reporters to produce scandal sheets and infotainment.

We had Dan Rostenskowski illegally selling his supply of free postage stamps a few years ago. That's the kind of story we love. Of course, it would have been even better if he were selling stamps to buy drugs.

Too many of our stories, even on Congress, veer off from the interesting, the useful, the important. What would you know about Strom Thurmond if you read the papers lately? Do we get any real serious attention to the fact that this man is third in line to succeed the president? Any serious coverage of what this man stands for, or what this man has done in his half-century in the Senate? No, what we get is "Isn't he cute" coverage.

These concerns mirror those found in a 1999 national study of reporters, conducted by the Pew Research Center, which found that most reporters (56%) think their profession tries to inflate personal and political scandals and that 67% agree that the media are devolving from information providers to infotainers.[21]

As for strengths of congressional coverage, many reporters cited its fairness. Perhaps inspired by the purported purpose of the survey, a number of reporters mentioned the lack of bias in coverage of Congress and the evenhanded manner in which both sides are portrayed.

I think we do a very good job of being even handed. I don't think anyone seriously believes that the press corps as a whole favors the Democrats or the Republicans. I mean Republicans complain about it, but I think they really just want to use that to get attention.

Read a day's, a month's, a year's worth of coverage, and I think you will see some of the same things in almost every paper. Both sides given a chance to state their position, a fair account of what has happened, in straight reporting almost no indication of which side the reporter thinks is right.

Other reporters suggested that covering Congress was one of the toughest jobs in political reporting; thus, the sheer production of information needs to be recognized.

You have 535 political operations on the Hill, all trying to produce positive headlines. Try to keep track of them, and every issue they're on, try just to keep track of every committee. This is a whole other world from other beats. You cover the president, you are covering one person, who often mentions a grand total of one public issue in a day.

THE STATE OF CONGRESS

Despite their strong assertions of fairness, reporters do not necessarily hold much regard for the Congress. As illustrated in Table 4.2, reporters generally do not think that members of Congress think for themselves or care very much about their constituents. Reporters' overall grade for Congress is displayed in Table 4.3.

As one of the reporters we interviewed noted, however, there is a similarity between reporters and the general public in this area:

Reporter C: People don't like Congress, but they like their Congressman. Most reporters have serious doubts about the Congress, but I would have trouble naming a single colleague who didn't admire one of them.

Table 4.2
Reporters' Opinion of Congress

	% agree
Members of Congress too often do not think for themselves	78
Members generally know or understand only a few issues	47
Members would rather get their names in the paper than get a bill passed	61
It is hard to get an honest answer from a member of Congress	56

N = 127.
Source: Authors' survey of congressional reporters.

Table 4.3
Reporters Grade Congress

A	9%
B	38%
C	30%
D	15%
F	8%
Average	C+

N = 127.
Source: Authors' survey of congressional reporters.

THE OUT-GROUP EFFECT

To what extent are reporters' perceptions influenced by their similarity to their target? To what extent are reporters displaying out-group-based thinking?

We tested for the influence of out-group thinking by asking reporters to rate Congress overall and individual members of Congress (both African American and white) on a series of traits that had been identified as being most crucial by congressional press staff (in Chapter 3) and identified in previous research as emblematic of congressional success (Mondak 1995). Specifically, we asked reporters to tell us whether certain members were hardworking, trustworthy, too partisan, open-minded, had the best interests of the country in mind, and were a credit to their profession. At the conclusion of the survey, we also asked reporters a few demographic questions, including their race. We can therefore consider whether race of reporter affects responses to Congress overall or responses to white and African American members of Congress.

As a further test, we also asked reporters to rate other reporters (both white and African American) on the same scale.

Racial Differences in Reporters' Evaluations of Congress?

Each reporter was asked to evaluate eight white members of Congress. The members were chosen for their prominence to ensure that the national sample of reporters would have impressions of each, and to balance partisanship and ideology. The most important and reliable comparison, though, is between white and African American reporters' responses to the same member. If the out-group effect is influencing their answers, whites should give these white representatives significantly higher scores.

As Table 4.4 reveals, in the vast majority of comparisons, whites were not significantly more positive toward these white members than were African American reporters. Comparing the ratings of individual members from whites and African Americans reveals that of 48 comparisons, only 6 have statistically significant differences, and in 1 of those it is the African American reporters who are more supportive of the white member. Taking Richard Gephardt (D-MO), for example, the consensus from both white and African American reporters is that he is hardworking and a credit to his profession, although smaller majorities of both groups of reporters see him as trustworthy or open-minded.

In addition to the overall rating, it is important to consider the standard deviation of each trait rating. A standard deviation is a measure of how much average change exists between responses. The higher the standard deviation, the more variation exists between each response. If every response is the same, for example, the standard deviation would be zero. Thus, the higher the standard deviation, the more consideration the reporters are giving to the traits of each individual member of Congress. The closer the standard deviation is to zero, the more the reporters are categorizing all these members with the same attributes. According to the out-group theory, the standard deviation should be higher for white reporters evaluating their in-group than for African American reporters who are evaluating their out-group. As the bottom row of Table 4.4 reveals, however, to the extent there is a difference, African American reporters have a higher standard deviation in their responses, suggesting they are making greater distinctions between members of their out-group — the opposite of what the theory suggests. Thus, the evaluation of white reporters offers no support to the out-group effect.

Table 4.4
Evaluation of White Members of Congress by Race of Reporter

	Hard-working	Trustworthy	Has Best Interests of Country in Mind	Too Partisan	Open Minded	Credit to Their Profession
Richard Gephardt	W 88 AA 91	W 69 AA 67	W 76 AA 80	W 84 AA 72*	W 60 AA 64	W 79 AA 85
Trent Lott	W 82 AA 77	W 60 AA 50*	W 61 AA 50*	W 87 AA 90	W 46 AA 39	W 64 AA 52*
Barbara Boxer	W 78 AA 79	W 65 AA 65	W 62 AA 67	W 88 AA 81	W 44 AA 49	W 66 AA 69
Tom Delay	W 85 AA 87	W 56 AA 49	W 57 AA 49*	W 91 AA 95	W 30 AA 30	W 58 AA 51
Kay Bailey Hutchinson	W 86 AA 82	W 82 AA 80	W 81 AA 83	W 68 AA 74	W 65 AA 60	W 84 AA 80
Dick Armey	W 83 AA 80	W 62 AA 50*	W 59 AA 51	W 90 AA 94	W 35 AA 31	W 62 AA 56
Tom Daschle	W 87 AA 87	W 70 AA 72	W 63 AA 69	W 78 AA 71	W 46 AA 51	W 74 AA 79
David Bonior	W 87 AA 82	W 71 AA 74	W 75 AA 75	W 80 AA 72	W 50 AA 56	W 75 AA 81
standard deviation	**W 3.3 AA 4.7**	**W 8 AA 12.2**	**W 9.1 AA 13.8**	**W 7.7 AA 10.3**	**W 11.6 AA 12.9**	**W 9 AA 14.1**

N = 127.
*p>.05
Source: Authors' survey of congressional reporters.

We also asked reporters to rate four African American members of Congress (Table 4.5). We asked for ratings of only four African Americans to decrease the likelihood that our interest in race would be obvious. Again, the responses from whites and African Americans are quite similar. Charles Rangel (D-NY), for example, is widely viewed by both groups of reporters as hardworking, trustworthy, and a credit to his profession. In only 4 of the 24 comparisons do African American reporters offer an evaluation that is significantly different from that of the white reporters. One of those cases features whites giving the African American representative the better score.

Nor does the standard deviation measure offer support to the out-group effect here. Rather than being consistently smaller, the out-group evaluation (white reporters on African American representatives) has a higher standard deviation on one measure and is equal on two others.

Table 4.5
Evaluation of African American Members of Congress by Race of Reporter

	Hard-working	Trust-worthy	Has Best Interests of Country in Mind	Too Partisan	Open Minded	Credit to Their Profession
John Conyers	W 88 AA 89	W 75 AA 81	W 71 AA 81*	W 84 AA 69*	W 57 AA 59	W 78 AA 84
Charles Rangel	W 91 AA 94	W 81 AA 88	W 77 AA 84	W 79 AA 69*	W 59 AA 61	W 85 AA 90
Maxine Waters	W 50 AA 52	W 42 AA 49	W 55 AA 61	W 88 AA 81	W 44 AA 50	W 41 AA 47
J.C. Watts	W 89 AA 86	W 70 AA 66	W 61 AA 56*	W 84 AA 89	W 40 AA 38	W 68 AA 66
standard deviation	W 19.7 AA 19.1	W 17.2 AA 17.3	W 9.8 AA 14	W 3.7 AA 9.7	W 9.4 AA 10.4	W 19.3 AA 19.3

N = 127.
* $p < .05$
Source: Authors' survey of congressional reporters.

Taken together, reporters' evaluation of Congress suggests that the race of the reporter is a minor to inconsequential factor and certainly fails to support the charge that reporters evaluate members and the Congress based on their racial closeness to representatives.

Racial Differences in Reporters' Evaluations of Reporters?

Examining reporter reaction to their peers is also quite instructive on this question. Just as we asked reporters to rate several members of Congress, we asked them to rate several prominent members of the fourth estate (Table 4.6). We attempted to fashion a list of reporters and media commentators with whom all our reporters would be familiar, and who had sufficient diversity to afford us the opportunity to make comparisons. As was the case in responding to members of Congress, again race apparently has little to do with the reporters' evaluations.

The differences in response to both white and African American reporters are negligible. In 48 comparisons of reaction to white reporters, only 2 gaps between white and African American ratings are statistically significant, and in 24 comparisons of African American reporters, only 1 is statistically significant. Bernard Shaw of CNN provides a clear illustration of the lack of significance of the race of the reporter, as he is nearly unanimously well rated by both white and African American reporters.

Out-group status also proves to be little related to the standard deviation of the media figure ratings. For most traits, whites did not make greater distinctions between white reporters than African Americans did, nor did African Americans make greater distinctions between African American reporters than whites did in any category.

Finally, we consider one other out-group possibility. Seeing the world as 'us versus them' could entail not just race but also profession. One manifestation of the out-group effect is that it can encourage people to see the greater value of members of their profession versus outsiders (Niven 1998, Chapter 4). We could, therefore, find evidence of out-group thinking if reporters see their profession as uniquely qualified for, among other things, politics. This possibility is suggested by the much higher evaluations reporters gave their colleagues than they gave members of Congress. Nevertheless, when we asked reporters if Congress would be better, and the American people better off, if more reporters were elected

Table 4.6
Evaluation of Reporters by Race of Reporter

	Hard-working	Trust-worthy	Has Best Interests of Country in Mind	Too Partisan	Open Minded	Credit to their profession
Jack Germond, *The Sun*	W 89 AA 90	W 90 AA 92	W 90 AA 94	W 23 AA 19	W 91 AA 94	W 95 AA 96
Bernie Shaw, CNN	W 91 AA 93	W 96 AA 98	W 98 AA 99	W 12 AA 7	W 95 AA 98	W 99 AA 99
Maureen Dowd, *New York Times*	W 91 AA 90	W 88 AA 85	W 82 AA 85	W 14 AA 17	W 95 AA 92	W 91 AA 88
Bob Woodward, *Washington Post*	W 79 AA 82	W 69 AA 76*	W 79 AA 82	W 14 AA 12	W 88 AA 89	W 89 AA 92
Clarence Page, *Chicago Tribune*	W 92 AA 90	W 94 AA 94	W 92 AA 96	W 16 AA 10	W 94 AA 97	W 96 AA 96
George Will, ABC/columnist	W 87 AA 83	W 86 AA 82	W 78 AA 74	W 29 AA 33	W 77 AA 72	W 85 AA 81
David Broder, *Washington Post*	W 93 AA 88	W 96 AA 96	W 95 AA 91	W 18 AA 14	W 90 AA 94	W 97 AA 95
Molly Ivins, *Fort Worth Star-Telegram*	W 90 AA 89	W 94 AA 95	W 90 AA 95*	W 27 AA 22	W 84 AA 89	W 92 AA 95
Bob Herbert, *New York Times*	W 89 AA 92	W 94 AA 96	W 91 AA 95	W 21 AA 12*	W 90 AA 98	W 96 AA 98
Dan Rather, CBS	W 85 AA 87	W 96 AA 94	W 97 AA 97	W 10 AA 8	W 98 AA 98	W 98 AA 98
Dewayne Wickham, *USA TODAY*	W 84 AA 87	W 89 AA 91	W 90 AA 95	W 20 AA 13	W 92 AA 94	W 95 AA 98
Sam Donaldson, ABC	W 81 AA 83	W 84 AA 88	W 90 AA 86	W 29 AA 26	W 80 AA 83	W 84 AA 87
standard deviation (White Reporters)	W 4.9 AA 3.3	W 8.8 AA 7	W 7.5 AA 7.7	W 7.5 AA 8	W 7.2 AA 8.1	W 5.2 AA 5.7
standard deviation (African American Reporters)	W 3.5 AA 2.6	W 2.9 AA 2.9	W 3.6 AA 1.8	W 4.1 AA 2.6	W 2.2 AA 1.8	W 1.7 AA 1.2

N = 127.
*p<.05
Source: Authors' survey of congressional reporters.

to Congress, the vast majority said no. Seventy-four percent of reporters disagreed with the notion that we should elect more reporters.[22]

What's wrong with that idea? Plenty. Most people I work with don't like having an editor, much less submitting their ideas to 400 odd other people for approval. You are talking about a profession that's born and bred for watching, not doing.

Reporters do not think all the world's problems would be solved if only more people like themselves were in charge. Nor do reporters evince a racially influenced evaluation pattern when commenting on white members of Congress, African American members of Congress, or white and African American members of the media. Given this apparent lack of out-group thinking, why, then, is media coverage strongly racialized? We turn to the distribution effect, the psychological influence of the relative numerical distinctiveness of African American representatives, for an alternative answer.

THE DISTRIBUTION EFFECT

The distribution effect creates assumptions based on the difference between a person and those who typically occupy that person's occupation. The distribution effect thus influences those who are least exposed to the distribution in question. In other words, reporters should be most affected where African American elected officials are rarest. Reporters in these areas should be most likely to stereotype based on the distribution of officeholders.

Therefore, to differentiate between reporters who work in cities where African American representatives are most unusual from those who work in areas that have a more established African American political history, we consider three indicators. First, are there multiple African American representatives serving in the paper's circulation area? Second, has an African American ever been elected to Congress from the paper's home state? Third, we include significant officials outside Congress by noting whether the paper's home state has had a major city run by an African American mayor. The three indicators suggest whether African American elected officials have had an opportunity to establish themselves versus having either no African American participation or so little that it can be considered a fluke. We include the mayoral measure to acknowledge the centrality of the local executive to many American newspapers, as the election of an African American city leader would presumably dim the uniqueness (and any associated inappropriateness) of an African American representative.

Among those reporters, white and African American, whose region has multiple African American representatives, overall scores for the African American politicians are somewhat higher (average of 4% higher positive response). What is even more notable, however, is the greater standard deviation associated with the responses of those from the higher-distribution cities (Table 4.7). In all six categories, there is a higher standard deviation among the high-distribution reporters, and correspondingly, greater homogenization from those in the low-distribution cities. In other words, those in high-distribution cities appear to more strongly consider the individual traits of the African American leaders they are evaluating, while those in low-distribution cities tend to lump the African American leaders together. This is the very essence of bias — the unwillingness to recognize the unique properties of members of a group. Those in low-distribution cities, which, to be clear, include both African American and white reporters, appear to be subject to the default picture of what a representative is like and respond to the uniqueness of African Americans by slightly downgrading their evaluation and by portraying them with a very broad brush.

The same pattern is repeated with regard to a distribution measure based on the lower thresholds of whether an African American has ever

Table 4.7
Standard Deviation of African American Member Ratings by Number of African American Representatives in Reporter's Region

	Hard-working	Trust-worthy	Has Best Interests of Country in Mind	Too Partisan	Open Minded	Credit to Their Profession
Zero or one	18.1	15.5	8.1	3.5	7.7	15.8
multiple	22.3	18.1	14.9	10.5	11.2	22.9

N = 127.
Source: Authors' survey of congressional reporters.

served in Congress or whether an African American mayor has ever been elected in the paper's home state (Tables 4.8, 4.9). In each case, reporters in the high distribution areas rate African American members more highly (average 3% and 5%, respectively) and reveal consistently greater variation in their responses to these African American officials.

Thus, support for the distribution effect is consistent with each of the three indicators of African American political presence. Where African Americans are a bigger part of the political scene, they are more likely to be judged positively by reporters and more likely to be judged based on their individual traits. Where African Americans are statistically less prevalent in office, they are more likely to be lumped together based on the reporter's understanding of holding office as a white avocation.

The logic of the distribution effect is quite clear. Imagine two Little Leaguers placed on a major league baseball team. Could you tell the two children apart in terms of their skills? Probably not, because their difference from the norm would be so overwhelming that you would lose the ability to differentiate between the two of them. The same process can take place in Congress. Reporters in higher-distribution areas, again both white and African American reporters, seem more cognizant of the details, the fine lines, of African American members because these members do not represent great political oddities to them; they appear neither completely unique nor out of place. Reporters in low-distribution cities, on the other hand, see a politics of white members in which African Americans are clearly numerically out of sync and therefore hard to distinguish. The distribution effect finding is consistent with Galtung and

Table 4.8

Standard Deviation of African American Member Ratings by Whether African American Representatives have Served in Paper's Home State

	Hard-working	Trust-worthy	Has Best Interests of Country in Mind	Too Partisan	Open Minded	Credit to Their Profession
No	17.8	15.7	9.9	4.8	7.1	13.1
Yes	24.4	18.5	15.7	9.5	12	23.8

N = 127.
Source: Authors' survey of congressional reporters.

Table 4.9
Standard Deviation of African American Member Ratings by Whether Reporter's State has Elected African American Mayor

	Hard-working	Trust-worthy	Has Best Interests of Country in Mind	Too Partisan	Open Minded	Credit to Their Profession
No	19.2	17.5	9.5	5.6	7.9	17.5
Yes	21.4	18.1	13.4	8.3	11.1	20.9

N = 127.
Source: Authors' survey of congressional reporters.

Ruge's (1970) analysis that suggests that two of the fundamental factors in media reaction to political events are familiarity and cultural proximity.

The distribution effect helps account for the pattern Representative William Clay (D-MO) finds in the media, which is that "the average reporter, white and black, covers legislative matters by ignoring the expertise of black members" on the vast range of topics not directly related to race.[23]

Reporter Reaction to Distribution Effect

The reporters we interviewed were generally dismissive of the claim that racialized coverage exists or is important. Nevertheless, after the results of the survey were in, we asked the ten reporters for their comments, and they were largely willing to entertain the possibility that the distribution effect influences media output.

Reporter D: I think that's a much more sensible answer than racism or some kind of overt prejudice. What you are basically saying is that the lack of familiarity with the situation causes some sloppy assumptions. It would certainly explain our fascination when someone is the first black elected to an office.

Nevertheless, a number maintained their steadfast position that there exists no problem, which therefore demands no explanation.

Reporter B: You can't tell me that I think . . . the way I write . . . is that a Congressman should be white. What my image of the ideal Congressman is has nothing to do with race.

LIMITATIONS OF THE DATA

Despite the protestations of the last reporter, support for the distribution effect appears strong. However, the limitations of the data should be acknowledged and explored. Among the most relevant threats to validity in a study such as this are demand characteristics (where people give the answers they think researchers want to hear) and social desirability (where people give the answers they think make them look best).

As has been mentioned, to make race a less prominent aspect of the survey and to make these problems less of a threat, respondents were told from the outset that this was a study of partisan bias in the media. More importantly, as has been noted throughout, our questions were not directly about race, and when we asked for reactions to African American figures, it was always in the context of asking about even more whites. Moreover, the diversity of targets used in this effort makes both demand characteristics and social desirability seem unlikely. Reporters' responses did not suggest the out-group effect when evaluating white members, African American members, white and African American reporters, or reporters as a whole. Meanwhile, support for the distribution effect is found with three different operationalizations of high distribution. Therefore, it is unlikely that reporters were altering their answers to conform to our interests or to protect their own image.

SUMMARY AND CONCLUSION

The product of the congressional media is racialized in that whites are more positively portrayed, more likely to be associated with a diverse agenda, and less likely to be shown as marginal players in the Capitol. Nothing in the behavior of African American politicians seems to account for this coverage, and their priorities and press efforts suggest a diversity of concerns and depth of effort and understanding that are belittled by the media. We therefore ask in this chapter whether the attitudes of the media create this racialized coverage.

We find, first, that the reporters we spoke to do not perceive that there is a racialized coverage problem in existence. Nor does our national survey of reporters suggest that the race of reporters determines how they view members of Congress. Support is found, however, for the distribution effect, a psychological process in which those whose traits are numerically rare in an occupation are viewed less favorably and less variably. In other words, reporters in areas with few African American representatives may be categorizing African Americans as political oddities, and this perception may encourage reporters to dismiss their value and fail to detect meaningful differences between the individual members of the group.

Racialized coverage, therefore, comes not from members themselves but from a distribution biased media. Bias in the media can be particularly pernicious, as Byrd (1997) argues, because the media's assumptions are self-perpetuating. Byrd cautions that reporters' stereotypes begin to seem accurate when the ideas they hold appear in others' coverage. Thus, when a reporter with a stereotypic assumption writes a story based on those assumptions, other reporters read that work and find further substantiation for their own stereotypes. Media stereotypes are, therefore, a monster capable of feeding itself.

NOTES

1. The obvious advantage of comparing members from the same area of the country is that it allows us to minimize the possibility that differences in media coverage simply reflect regional variations in journalistic practices. Additionally, both members are relatively junior (Wynn was elected in 1992; Moran in 1990). Both, in fact, served on the House International Relations Committee. While Wynn has sustained a somewhat more liberal voting record than Moran, their ideological differences have not been particularly significant.

2. *Washington Post*, October 29, 1994.

3. Ibid.

4. *Washington Post*, October 1, 1994.

5. *Washington Post*, May 7, 1995.

6. *Washington Post*, August 23, 1993.

7. Romer, Jamieson, and Coteau (1998) find, for example, that African Americans are overrepresented in coverage of criminals, while whites are overrepresented in coverage of victims. In other words, as the exaggerated representation of African American criminals paints a distinct and negative picture, the sympathetic portrayal of white victims suggests their universality.

8. New York Times, April 9, 1998. A 1998 ASNE survey reported 89% of the newspaper workforce was white, with approximately 5% African American.

9. *New York Times*, April 9, 1998.

10. Ibid.

11. *New York Times*, April 3, 1998.

12. According to Clay (1992) and Duncan and Lawrence (1997), 23 states have sent African Americans to the House or Senate: Alabama, California, Connecticut, Florida, Georgia, Illinois, Indiana, Louisiana, Maryland, Massachusetts, Michigan, Mississippi, Missouri, New Jersey, New York, North Carolina, Ohio, Oklahoma, Pennsylvania, South Carolina, Tennessee, Texas, Virginia.

13. Authors' calculation based on data in Clay (1992).

14. Ibid.

15. *New York Times*, April 3, 1998.

16. Reporters were told that their responses would be kept confidential. Each reporter is identified with a letter in the text:

Reporter A	African American	Southern Newspaper
Reporter B	African American	Southern Newspaper
Reporter C	White	Northern Newspaper
Reporter D	White	Southern Newspaper
Reporter E	White	Western Newspaper
Reporter F	White	Midwestern Newspaper
Reporter G	African American	Midwestern Newspaper
Reporter H	African American	Midwestern Newspaper
Reporter I	African American	Northern Newspaper
Reporter J	White	Northern Newspaper

17. The list was obtained through a colleague working in the House staff.

18. Using $p<.05$ as a standard.

19. Dates and Barlow (1993) compiled a list of African American journalists.

20. All data have been weighted to correct for the oversample of African American reporters.

21. "Striking the Balance: Audience Interests, Business Pressures, and Journalists' Values," report of the Pew Research Center for the People and the Press, 1999. (See also Hess 1994; Parker 1994).

22. Mike Schneider, formerly of ABC News, unsuccessfully sought a House seat in New Jersey in 1998. Scott Klug, a former local television reporter, served in the House from 1991 to 1999.

23. Correspondence with authors, September 29, 1999.

5

The Electoral Effects of Racialized Coverage

"It is an undeniable fact of life that what is read, seen, and heard in the white-controlled media has indelibly molded opinions and perpetrated negative images in and about the black community," said Representative William Clay (D-MO), speaking to the Congressional Black Caucus' hearing on "Racism in the Media" in 1972.

Clay reprinted the comments in his 1992 book on African American members of Congress, not to celebrate how much things have changed but to decry how little progress has occurred. Media bias against African American leaders, according to Clay, "has not abated in recent years. If anything, it has intensified" (1992, 337).

Indeed, Clay claims that African American members of Congress can expect "harassment" and "vicious press assaults" (1992, 319) and that he personally has been the victim of "certain elements of the media . . . engaged in a concerted effort to deny me re-election, to publicly ridicule and embarrass me, and most of all, to send me to the penitentiary" (1992, 323).

Ultimately, Clay argues, this coverage has the effect of undermining the political careers of African Americans.

Does the racialized coverage that we have found and that Clay decries really hurt the electoral standing of African American representatives? Does it perhaps help them by fostering a mistreated, outsider persona that might appeal to their constituents? Or, might there be no tangible effect at all?

We have documented a tendency of the media to treat African American leaders differently, and we have noted that such coverage does not seem to flow directly from the politicians and that stereotypes in the media can be linked to the distribution effect — assumptions spawned by the ubiquity of whites in office and relative rarity of African Americans. However, does any of this coverage matter to the representatives' political futures?

MINIMAL EFFECTS HYPOTHESES

Any News is Good News

Research on the role of media coverage in congressional elections has been greatly influenced by the notion that representatives seek coverage to facilitate reelection. Parker (1981) argues that awareness is the key to congressional candidate success, and the media are the dominant mechanism by which to attain mass awareness. Payne (1980) believes that insecure members of Congress are more likely to seek publicity, presumably to help their reelection efforts. Goidel and Shields (1994) illustrate the positive relationship between constituent media use and support for incumbents. Goidel and Shields conclude that media exposure tends to bias voters toward incumbents. What all these studies (and a considerable number of others) have in common is a foundation on the assertion that media coverage is inherently beneficial (see also Clarke and Evans 1983; Paletz and Entman 1981; Cook 1986). Toward that end, Maisel recounts the conclusion of many congressional challengers he interviewed: "newspaper coverage" that continually mentioned the incumbent "was the hardest part of running" as a challenger (1982, 117).

No News Is Good News

Alternatively, some have come to the direct opposite conclusion, that is, more media attention can be harmful to incumbent health (Niven and Zilber 1998). Specifically, national media attention has been linked to decreases in incumbent popularity in the 1990s. Given the advantage in campaign spending that an incumbent typically has (and the attendant television ads and direct mail pieces those dollars buy), less media coverage actually translates into greater control for the member over the images seen. Using a measure of national prominence, based on media attention garnered by all incumbents running for reelection in 1990-1996, revealed that heavy national coverage translated into a loss of support of up to eight points for the most heavily covered members of the House of Representatives.

No One Is Paying Attention

Reaching the same conclusion but with a different rationale would be those who argue that the media are relatively unimportant to elections. Some find that voters pay selective attention to news, taking in material that they already agree with, while discounting or ignoring information that is contrary to their feelings (McGuire 1985). Others argue that the media are incapable of changing our political preferences because we simply pay too little attention and understand too little of what we are told about politics on the news (Neuman 1986; MacKuen 1984). Further, some would claim that the media's coverage of politics is simply too insubstantial to have much effect on vote choice (Patterson and McClure 1976). Ultimately, Neuman (1986) concludes, the media are unable to convey pertinent information in such a way that the audience can remember and use it.

All three of these perspectives suggest that the media will have little effect on African American representatives. Whether more coverage helps or hurts, given that the media are as likely to cover African American members as white members, either perspective implies that racialized media coverage should not have a significant effect on African American electoral popularity. Concomitantly, if the media have almost no electoral effect on voters, again that suggests African American representatives will not be adversely affected by the distinct pattern of media coverage they receive.

EMPOWERMENT EFFECT HYPOTHESIS

In contrast to the previous arguments, some researchers believe that the scope of effect the media have varies tremendously by the attributes of the observer (Entman 1989). Specifically, many who study racial politics believe that the political perspectives of African Americans will lead them to have a quite distinct reaction to media coverage (Davis and Gandy 1999).

African American voters are in a unique position of perceiving the importance of government in providing for their needs, while simultaneously feeling a general distrust for a government run by, and potentially for, whites (Swain 1995). Scholars have argued that as African Americans attempt to find outlets to prevent being overwhelmed by white influences and power, their efforts can produce vastly different perspectives on politics (Levine 1977). This fear of being overwhelmed is evident in Sigelman and Welch's (1991, 52-53) findings, for example, that 82% of African Americans believe there is at least a "fair amount" of white prejudice against them and that 25% of African Americans believe a majority of whites accept the racial views of the KKK. Sigelman and Welch conclude, "It is clear that blacks see racial discrimination as an everyday occurrence, not an historical curiosity" (1991, 59).

Meanwhile, a sizable majority of African Americans believe that the government is not doing enough to ensure equality (Sigelman and Welch 1991, 138). Toward that end, where they are a politically relevant force, members of minority communities can be expected to practice "racially conscious politics" as part of an effort to assert their groups' position (Huckfeldt and Kohfeld 1989). This creates a special relationship between minority voters and minority representatives. Kleppner argues that African American candidates can be seen by African American voters as a "means of political liberation" (1985, 154). Minority representation facilitates feeling not only protected but also valued as a community (Swain 1995; Pettigrew and Alston 1988).

This desire for representation among African Americans can create intense devotion. Swain quotes one African American member of the House as saying, "One of the advantages and disadvantages of representing blacks is their shameless loyalty to their incumbents. You can almost get away with raping babies and be forgiven. You don't have any vigilance about your performance" (1995, 73).

Bobo and Gilliam (1993) argue that racially conscious politics emerge in minority communities with high political empowerment. Empowerment is important, they theorize, because it increases levels of political trust, political efficacy, and the desire for political knowledge. Bobo and Gilliam, indeed, find higher levels of empowerment (which produces citizens who are more engaged in politics and more knowledgeable about government) where African American voters are represented by African American officials.

Given this line of thinking, a number of studies have suggested that African Americans will feel empowered by, and react positively to, coverage of African American representatives, while having much less commitment to white representatives and no positive response to coverage of white representatives (Sniderman, Swain, and Elms 1995; Jones and Clemons 1993; McCormack and Jones 1993; Sears, Citrin, and Kosterman 1987; Cavanaugh 1983).

RACIAL PRIMING HYPOTHESIS

Taking the empowerment hypothesis one step further, some analysts believe the media can "prime" voters to evaluate their political leaders based on certain issues and images the media focus on (McCombs and Shaw 1977). In short, when the media cover a politician on a certain issue, voters are encouraged to create a linkage between the politician and the issue. That linkage resurfaces when the voter evaluates the politician — such that the voter sees the politician in terms of the heavily covered issue and reacts to the politician based on the voter's connection to that issue.

In this context, continual coverage of African American members' racial focus will prime voters to define African American representatives based on racial issues. Importantly, such a process can potentially have both positive and negative ramifications. A priming association can link a leader with a popular and successful notion, just as it can link a leader with a damaging position.

President George Bush, for example, in 1991 benefited from priming when the media's focus was on the Gulf War, considered by most voters to be a terrific success. By 1992, however, when the media's focus had shifted away from the war and to the economy, voters were reminded to link Bush with an issue on which he was considered by many to have floundered.

Moreover, priming on the very same issue can have both positive and negative effects, depending on the disposition of the individual voters. For African American representatives, heavy coverage on racial affairs could have the effect of creating a positive issue prime for African American voters, while simultaneously creating a negative prime for white voters.

The research of Giles and Evans (1987) illustrates the significance of white reaction to threats to their political power. In situations where white political power is compromised, we can expect whites to react very negatively to African Americans' political reach. Thus, the most prominent reaction to racialized coverage could be found among whites with African American representatives — reacting negatively to coverage of African American-centered political power.[1]

Reeves (1997) demonstrates the effect of priming in racialized coverage in an experimental setting. Reeves created a fictitious, two-candidate race for mayor in which respondents were read a newspaper article describing the campaign. The article focused either on the environment or on affirmative action. The mayoral candidates were identified in the article as either white or black. Reeves found that when the article focused on the nonracial environmental issue, respondents were prone to favor the African American candidate. Their choice appeared unrelated to their preferences on a variety of racial issues and beliefs. When the article instead focused on affirmative action, the African American candidate's lead disappeared, and responses were strongly influenced by racial attitudes. Respondents, thus, did not always react to race; they reacted to race when it was the focus of the article, when it was made to be their focus by media coverage. As Citrin, Green, and Sears (1990) have argued, race matters most when it represents a salient threat.

According to the racial priming argument, there should be a wide gap between African American and white reaction to African American representatives. Moreover, since white representatives are not portrayed with an exclusive focus on white concerns, African American voters should be more accepting of white representatives than white voters will be of African American representatives.

SURVEY INFORMATION

To gauge the effect of racialized coverage, we turn to the National Election Studies data from 1994, 1996, and 1998, the three election cycles during which we analyzed media coverage. In each year, the NES asked respondents to rate congressional candidates on a feeling thermometer. The feeling thermometer is a 100-point scale, with 0 the strongest negative response, 100 the strongest positive response, and 50 meaning a neutral response. We use the feeling thermometer as our main measure of evaluation of congressional incumbents and challengers.

Feeling thermometers are popular in analyzing assessments of Congress because they are meaningful even when the incumbent faces no opposition or token opposition. Unlike actual vote choice, which will be influenced, in many cases dictated, by the existence and strength of the opposition, everyone can offer a positive or negative evaluation of his or her incumbent, regardless of the strength of the opposition.[2] Ultimately, scholars have argued that even apart from the strength of the opposition concern, feeling thermometers are superior to vote choice in indicating the voters' utility for the candidate (Page and Jones 1979; Markus and Converse 1979; Kenney and Rice 1984).

To avoid attempting to explain situations outside the scope of this study, we have selected for analysis only white and African American respondents who are represented by either white or African American Democrats in Congress. We have chosen to rely exclusively on Democrats to provide us with meaningful comparisons for analysis. There are, obviously, occasions where respondents represented by African American Republicans are not even found in these surveys, and the dearth of African Americans represented by white Republicans similarly precludes useful analysis.

We analyze, then, four groups: white voters represented by whites, white voters represented by African Americans, African American voters represented by African Americans, and African American voters represented by whites. Within these four groups are the crucial comparisons that will suggest how serious the effects of racialized coverage are and to whom they apply.

Overview of Hypotheses

Following the implications of previously described research, we explore three plausible ramifications of racialized media coverage of Congress.

First, applying the findings suggesting either that the amount of coverage matters or that the media have relatively little effect in this process, we should expect to see little difference in media effects on white and African American voters or white and African American members.

Second, applying the empowerment findings suggests that African American voters should react quite positively to African American members and negatively to white members and that added attention to media coverage should serve to widen this gap.

Third, applying the priming argument suggests that African American members should be much more popular with African American voters than with white voters. Meanwhile, white members should suffer no such penalty from African American voters.

RESULTS

The Lack of Media Effect

One possibility that would suggest that the media's racialized coverage has little effect would be if white and African American members achieved similar popularity levels. Indeed, between 1994 and 1998, the average feeling thermometer rating of white Democratic incumbents is 60, while the average feeling thermometer rating of African American Democratic incumbents is 61. On the surface, hardly the grist for great charges of bias. Moreover, examining the job approval of incumbent House Democrats also shows strong similarity, with white Democrats achieving 82% approval, and African American Democrats, 80% approval.

Perhaps reaction to these members is affected by the media, but this effect is masked by the relative feelings for Republicans in the sample. For example, if voters represented by whites are more pro-Republican than the voters evaluating African Americans, perhaps their ultimate similarity in evaluation of the Democratic incumbent reflects the result of the media's pulling up the scores of white Democratic members and depressing the scores of African American Democratic members. In other words, the general inclination of those evaluating African American representatives might be more pro-Democratic; therefore the scores for their representative should be higher but are not.

To explore this possibility, we calculated feeling thermometer scores for the Republican House challengers in these same districts. These are candidates with whom respondents generally have little contact, and who are therefore largely evaluated in terms of their party. Here, respondents from white member districts rate the Republican challenger with a 52, while respondents from African American member districts rate their Republican challenger with a 53. Such a result suggests the similarity of the respondents who are evaluating white and African American members and therefore reinforces the notion that white and African American members are equally popular and not significantly affected by the media.

Such a conclusion is not supported when the results are broken down to consider the race of the respondent, however. As Table 5.1 reveals, the popularity of white and African American members is the product of vastly different responses from white and African American voters. African American members are strongly supported by their African American constituents, while falling on the disliked side of the scale when rated by white voters. Such wide differences cast doubt on the notion that the media have little effect.

The Effect of Empowerment

The same results also undercut the empowerment hypothesis. Rather than African American voters resoundingly supporting African American representatives and revealing indifference for white representatives, Table 5.1 shows that African American voters give their representatives nearly the same score, whether the official is African American or white. Indeed, African Americans offer stratospheric job approval ratings (Table 5.2) to their white representatives, ratings that are actually higher than those offered by African American voters to African American representatives. If African Americans were empowered by African American representation and coverage of it, they should embrace African American members and should respond much more strongly to African American members than to white members.

Racial Priming

While the data presented thus far do not support the minimal effects or empowerment hypotheses, voter reaction is completely consistent with racial priming. For example, white voters offer support to white representatives, while giving African American representatives a negative score (Table 5.1).

This pattern is quite consistent with racialized coverage. African American members get coverage that suggests they are interested only in African American concerns and coverage that emphasizes that they are locked out of the power structure. To white voters, this coverage primes them to think of their representative in racial terms, which suggests to whites that they are not important to their representative and should not expect their representative to work for them, or successfully address their concerns.

Table 5.1
Constituent Ratings of Incumbent House Democrats

	1998	1996	1994	Mean
white voter/ white representative (n=1,067)	63	59	57	59
white voter/ African American representative (n=89)	47	55	47	49
African American voter/ African American representative (n=119)	74	70	69	71
African American voter/ white representative (n=133)	67	66	71	69

Note: Cell entries are mean feeling thermometer ratings on a scale of 0 (lowest rating) to 100 (highest positive rating).
Source: National Election Studies, 1994-1998.

Significantly, white representatives suffer from no such problem reaching their out-group, African American voters. White representatives, in contrast to African American members, do not receive coverage that primes voters to think they exclude anyone. Their coverage, which suggests they work hard on a variety of issues, are more influential in Washington, and are better legislators than African Americans, conveys a positive message to all observers and results in positive ratings from both white and African American constituents.

This is a crucial distinction. White representatives and African American representatives wish to, and work hard to, communicate their concerns for all their constituency. The difference is that white members can actually receive coverage consistent with that image, while African Americans are likely to be portrayed as having a narrow focus on their own ethnic group. The result is white representatives who can effectively

Table 5.2
Job Approval of Incumbent House Democrats

	1998	1996	1994	Mean
white voter/ white representative (n=969)	88	80	74	80
white voter/African American representative (n=72)	58	71	64	64
African American voter/African American representative (n=116)	94	93	82	90
African American voter/ white representative (n=129)	100	94	96	97

Note: Cell entries are the percentage of respondents who approve of the job their incumbent representative is doing in office.
Source: National Election Studies, 1994-1998.

appeal to everyone and African Americans who can effectively appeal only to African Americans.

Job approval results offer the same pattern (Table 5.2) as the feeling thermometer scores. Again, African American representatives are widely lauded by African American constituents and much less likely to be endorsed by whites. White members, on the other hand, are supported by whites and nearly universally approved by their African American constituents!

These results make clear that this is not simply a case of voters rigidly responding to the race of the member — as African American voters are giving white representatives marks that are as high as, or higher than, those they give African American representatives. White voters, on the other hand, give strong approval only to white members.

Of course, one must consider the possibility that these numbers are driven by partisanship — that the likelihood of African Americans to support Democrats creates these patterns, rather than media coverage. Table 5.3, however, shows that African American respondents actually give the Republican House candidate a slightly higher rating than do whites. If partisanship does not result in lower scores when African Americans evaluate Republicans, it would seem unlikely that extreme partisanship is responsible for African Americans' support for Democrats.

Moreover, the white voters represented by African American members are by no means uniquely pro-Republican. These white respondents have the same reaction to Republicans as whites in white member districts and a lower score for Republicans than African Americans offered.

POLITICAL ATTENTION AND INCUMBENT RATINGS

While this pattern fits neatly with the racialized coverage explanation, can this result be linked to media usage? If, for example, there is no relationship between media use and support for representatives, it would hardly suggest that racialized media coverage is the root cause.

Table 5.3
Constituent Ratings of Republican House Challengers

	1998	1996	1994	Mean
white voter/ white representative (n=629)	50	50	53	51
white voter/ African American representative (n=39)	53	46	54	51
African American voter/ African American representative (n=53)	44	55	60	54
African American voter/ white representative (n=58)	63	49	55	53

Note: Cell entries are mean feeling thermometer ratings on a scale of 0 (lowest rating) to 100 (highest positive rating).
Source: National Election Studies, 1994-1998.

Attention to politics and ratings of Democratic incumbents are presented in Table 5.4. The table compares the mean feeling thermometer rating of the Democratic incumbent representatives provided by those who "pay a lot of attention," to politics and political coverage with the responses of those who are only somewhat interested in politics. Most notable is the contrast between whites represented by African Americans and African Americans represented by whites. Just as the racialized coverage pattern would suggest, white representatives are helped by increased interest and attention to politics, as African Americans who are very interested give their white representative a score seven points higher than those who are less interested. White representatives stand to gain in this situation, as any assumption an African American voter might make that the white member lacks interest in representing the entire district is assuaged by media coverage. African American representatives, conversely, lose eight points of support from their white constituents who are more attuned to politics compared to those who pay less attention. For African American representatives, the media sell the notion that they are

Table 5.4
Effect of Attention to Politics on Ratings of Incumbent House Democrats

	1994-1998 Mean
white voter/ white representative (n=1,067)	-3
white voter/African American representative (n=89)	-8
African American voter/African American representative (n=119)	0
African American voter/white representative (n=133)	+7

Note: Cell entries represent difference between feeling thermometer rating of those who report they pay a lot of attention to politics compared to those who respond that they are somewhat interested or less. A negative number indicates the very interested had a lower rating.
Source: National Election Studies, 1994-1998.

uninterested in whites, and whites who pay the most attention respond by turning against their member of Congress.

ELEMENTS OF SUPPORT FOR REPRESENTATIVES

While not asked in each survey, two questions that assess attributes of House candidates suggest some of the thinking behind the feeling thermometer and job approval ratings. In 1994 respondents were asked whether their representative was more interested in solving problems or gaining personal prestige. Given the tendency for the media to portray African American representatives as less powerful and less capable, one would expect this question to offer significant insight into what makes some whites uncomfortable with African American leaders.

Indeed, while African Americans represented by African Americans typically said they believed their member cared more about solving problems, whites represented by African Americans typically said their member placed a higher value on gaining personal attention rather than getting the job done (Table 5.5). For white representatives, again, no such contrast existed. Both white and African American voters, reflecting media that offer this portrayal, typically believed their white representative was interested in solving problems.

In 1998 respondents were asked whether their incumbent keeps in touch with the district, again, an area in which members of Congress would universally hope their constituents would recognize their commitment. But racialized coverage suggests to whites that African Americans do not keep in touch with their group; ergo, they do not do a very good job of keeping in touch with the district. Indeed, while most African Americans thought their African American representative did a "very good" job of keeping in touch with the district, no whites agreed with that sentiment when commenting on their African American representative. Again, for white representatives, the overwhelming majority of both white and African American constituents believed their representative kept in touch with the district (Table 5.6).

The data presented thus offer both consistent and considerable support for a priming effect from racialized coverage. Compare the reaction of African Americans who are represented by whites to the reaction of whites represented by African Americans: the former group rates their representative 20 points higher on the feeling thermometer, gives their representative a job approval rating 33 points higher, and increases their

Table 5.5
Democratic House Incumbent Interested in "Solving Problems" over Personal Prestige, 1994

	% who agree
white voter/ white representative (n=554)	59
white voter/African American representative (n=51)	39
African American voter/African American representative (n=45)	57
African American voter/ white representative (n=86)	67

Source: National Election Studies, 1994.

Table 5.6
Democratic House Incumbent "Kept in Touch with District," 1998

	% who agree member has done "very good" or "good" job of keeping in touch
white voter/ white representative (n=195)	75
white voter/African American representative (n=16)	19
African American voter/African American representative (n=33)	79
African American voter/ white representative (n=23)	92

Source: National Election Studies, 1998.

rating of the incumbent by 7 points among voters who pay attention to politics, while the latter group decreases their rating by 8 points among those paying attention. The former group is 28 points more likely to believe their representative is interested in solving problems and an astounding 73 points more likely to believe their representative keeps in touch with the district! Every one of these results suggests the effects of racial priming, where the message that African American representatives care only about race serves to warn whites that a vote for an African American is a vote against themselves.[3] Conversely, white representatives enjoy the fruits of media coverage that reminds African American voters about their large, varied, and inclusive agendas.

Contrast the extremes between these two groups with the much smaller differences between African Americans represented by African Americans and whites represented by whites. Again, consistent with racial priming, both African Americans represented by African Americans and whites represented by whites receive acceptable messages from the media, and both respond with support for their incumbents.

SOCIAL DESIRABILITY

Any user of survey questions involving sensitive areas such as race must consider the possibility of socially desirable answers. People could modify their responses to mask their true feelings, to offer what they think is the socially approved position. One must therefore be concerned whether questions on race and racism are eliciting socially acceptable responses rather than true responses.

Our confidence that whites are genuine in their lower ratings of African American representatives is strong, however, because it is the opposite of a socially desirable pattern. If whites were masking their feelings toward African Americans to hide their prejudice, then whites should give African American representatives equal, or even higher, ratings than African American voters do. As Fiske and Taylor argue, "When people are willing to break with norms or conventions . . . one can be reasonably certain that their behavior reflects their true beliefs because by so doing they are risking socially aversive consequences" (1991, 29). There is, as such, no reason to suspect that the patterns illustrated here are the product of misleading, socially desirable answering strategies.[4]

IMPLICATIONS OF RACIAL PRIMING

African American representatives are affected by racial priming. Due to the media's slanted portrayal of their priorities and legislative work, African American members have a harder time attracting white voter support than white members have garnering African American voter support. In most basic terms, the media bring extra voters to white representatives by priming African American voters to see them in inclusive terms, while the media shoe away white voters from African American representatives by priming voters to view them in exclusive terms.

For many members, the consequences of this pattern are admittedly slight. Members such as Bobby Rush (D-IL) and Major Owens (D-NY) represent districts that are overwhelmingly African American and can therefore be reelected ad infinitum without even a single white vote. Even if media coverage costs them the support of most white voters, there are barely enough white voters in these districts for the political effect to be seen.

However, this is of little comfort for the increasing number of African American members who represent districts with significant white populations or even majority-white populations. Sanford Bishop (D-GA) and Cynthia McKinney (D-GA) have been redistricted into areas that are no longer majority African American, and their political careers now depend on their ability to reach out to the white voter, to convince the white voter that they are suited for legislative work and that their agenda is inclusive, not exclusive. This is a task the media actively inhibits, as media coverage of African American members helps antagonize potentially crucial white voters.

Perhaps even more unsettling than the effect this media coverage has on African Americans running for the House, though, is the potential limitation such coverage places on their political careers. African American members of Congress have a very distinct career pattern. While many African Americans have achieved prodigious levels of support in their districts, providing them ample electoral security locally (Gerber 1996), not a single African American member of the House has ever been able to transfer his or her political power to a statewide electoral victory. That is, no African American member of the House has ever been able to secure a Senate seat or become governor. Why does this great disparity exist between success in their districts and closed doors outside their districts? Obviously, the political, ideological, and demographic differences between the typical districts represented by African Americans and the larger states in which those districts exist play an important part in this process. Another important culprit, however, is the media.

By continually mentioning race and ethnic issues, as well as the racial and ethnic identities of the members, the media are alienating the white voters whose support becomes essential in races for higher offices. As Terkildsen argues, this pattern of media coverage helps solidify African American representatives' position as "symbols of unsettling activism and fear for many whites" (1996, 3).

In 1996 Chip Pickering, a successful Republican candidate for the House in Mississippi, told voters in his district how important it was to elect him and a Republican majority, to keep certain unpalatable leaders out of power in the Congress. Pickering told his audience that these leaders did not have the country's interests at heart. The leaders he named, Charles Rangel (D-NY), Ronald Dellums (D-CA), and John Conyers (D-MI), are all African Americans.[5]

Ultimately, then, African Americans who wish to secure the votes of whites have to overcome the assertion that theirs is an agenda of exclusion and particularistic group benefits, an assertion advanced not only by racist candidates and their supporters but by the national media.

NOTES

1. Indeed, even use of the term "African American" can induce a defensively negative reaction among whites (Zilber and Niven 1995).

2. The limitations of using vote choice as a dependent variable are exacerbated because the National Elections Studies do not and cannot provide perfect representations of all types of races. Gow and Eubank (1984) find, for example, that in some years the NES has sampled too few districts with quality challengers, which can further restrict the variance with regard to voter preference for an incumbent.

3. Witt, Paget, and Matthews (1995, 238) cite a good example of the negative consequences of this assumption: Carol Moseley-Braun's pollster explained that her campaign could not talk about the generally very popular Head Start program, because white voters saw it as an issue Moseley-Braun cared about only to "help her own people."

4. To the extent that any social desirability pattern did exist in the answers, it would serve only to strengthen the support for the racial priming hypothesis.

5. *USA TODAY*, September 26, 1996.

6

Racialized Media Coverage: Conclusions and Implications

Asked to submit an essay on the "reality of Black America" in 1994, a student at North Hagerstown High School in Washington County, Maryland, authored the following passage:

The image of Blacks is mostly not created through cases where Blacks occur in the media, but where they do not occur. For example, as we watch TV, we see a great deal of black athletes. But while 60% of all football-players are black, there are only two (!) black coaches in football. How does this influence the image of Blacks? Obviously, it leads us to think of Blacks as being good in sports rather than being good at organizing and managing. The fact that the latter is much more valued in our society adds to the destructiveness of this notion. Blacks are seen to be good at sports, music, comedy, and cheap TV shows, and are seldom representatives of the more valued skills of our society, like verbal or mathematical intelligence or historical or scientific knowledge. In summary, we can say that Blacks do not appear in the media as they should. If they do, then often within a negative context. This indicates that in the field of media, as in the society as a whole, change is needed to show what Blacks are truly capable of (in a positive way), and thereby preventing a wrong and inferior or even hateful image of them.[1]

The student's poignant argument is, in essence, a microcosm of our own: the image of blacks is not created through cases where blacks occur in the media, but where they do *not* occur. What is so troubling is not that

African Americans in Congress are frequently portrayed as concerned about minorities but how *infrequently* they are portrayed as typical members of Congress whose concerns parallel those of the majority.

SUMMARY OF RESULTS AND IMPLICATIONS

The coupling of press secretary interviews with a systematic content analysis paints a stark portrait of congressional media coverage. Although similar in quantity, coverage of African American members is substantively different. African Americans are significantly more likely to be identified by race, mentioned in stories involving racial issues, and portrayed as Washington outsiders whose day-to-day activities and overall goals are defined by a narrow range of constituent interests.

There appear to be no plausible explanations for this pattern other than race. Partisan affiliation, ideology, and seniority certainly do not account for the discrepancy; whites with political backgrounds similar to those of African Americans receive coverage that is much closer to that of other whites than African Americans. We also find no evidence from the members' Web pages to suggest that African Americans are willfully projecting the sorts of race-centric images seen in the news.

At least indirectly, our analysis confirms suspicions that the media are primarily responsible for creating unwarranted stereotypical images. Accustomed to seeing predominantly white faces in positions of authority, many reporters appear willing to mentally lump African American members into a single, amorphous category with virtually indistinguishable and interchangeable components. Set apart from the rest of the House by a glaring physical idiosyncrasy, one is much the same as another.

By eliminating the only other potential source of stereotypical news images — the members themselves — we would feel confident in reaching this conclusion even in the absence of additional supporting evidence. But the conclusion is reinforced by what we heard directly from reporters themselves. Racialized news coverage barely seems to have entered the media's collective consciousness, as few reporters expressed even the slightest concern that coverage of African Americans may focus too heavily on race. Confronted directly with the potential harm that may result from racialized coverage, reporters were apt to dodge responsibility by falling back on the "it's true" defense, which we take as further support for our inferences. Considered in its entirety, our evidence paints a clear picture of racialized media coverage, with little room for interpretation.

Perhaps the study's most important finding is that racialized media coverage presents more than an abstract theoretical problem. To the contrary, there are significant real-world implications. While incumbents in minority districts may be reaping short-term electoral benefits, racialized coverage may well account for African Americans' persistent inability to translate impressive district support into statewide or national political standing. Time and time again we see white representatives parlay their House seats into successful statewide campaigns, while popular African American members are summarily dismissed as "local" politicians who stand no chance of achieving higher office.

Cynical as this prevailing conventional wisdom might be, our findings support its underlying accuracy. By making it virtually impossible to appeal to moderate white voters who do not necessarily share minorities' goals, racialized news encourages African American representatives to restrict their political ambitions to indefinite reelection.

This subtle effect is easily overlooked by reporters and researchers and perhaps even the minority members themselves. It is easily overlooked because African Americans have steadily gained seats in the House and because minority members usually enjoy tremendous electoral support — often winning reelection by enormous margins. It is therefore tempting to conclude that media coverage of African Americans cannot possibly be harmful. According to this logic, whatever media bias exists must favor African Americans, so why would African Americans need to complain?

Unfortunately, many do not. Like most members of Congress, African Americans are often myopically focused on their next election. If it looks to be an easy victory in November, then there is seemingly nothing to complain about.

However, our findings suggest otherwise. To put it bluntly, African American members enjoy tremendous electoral success only because their districts are populated by voters who view racialized news as good news. The fact that white voters appear to be turned off by this same coverage is not likely to be seen as a problem by politicians who do not depend on their votes.

But this strategy has surely helped to keep African American politicians from reaching higher office and threatens to keep them out for many years to come. Moreover, with the Supreme Court having ruled that race can no longer be the sole factor in determining district boundaries,

African Americans who wish to remain in the House may soon find that their political lives depend on their ability to attract white voters. For many, then, the same racialized coverage that once helped ensure easy reelection will suddenly present a formidable electoral obstacle.

To use a final sports analogy: throughout the 1990s African Americans eagerly padded their win totals by scheduling lots of easy home games against weak opposition. This strategy may get them into the play-offs once in a while, but a good coach realizes you cannot win a championship unless you also know how to beat tough opponents on the road. Racialized media coverage will leave many African Americans unprepared for the tough road games ahead, which may ultimately prevent them from ever winning a political championship.

SUGGESTIONS

One of the most common complaints leveled against academic research is that it frequently points out problems without recommending any concrete solutions. While this tack is often used as a means of dismissing or ignoring valid criticisms, we agree that academics should do more to help solve the problems their research uncovers. With this in mind, we turn now to suggestions for minimizing racialized media coverage of Congress.

Media

To their credit, most journalists seem willing to acknowledge problems associated with covering minorities. Page through any recent book on journalism ethics, and you are likely to come across several strategies for increasing diversity in the newsroom. To ensure that minority issues receive more coverage, most urge news organizations to hire more minority reporters and editors and to pay closer attention to the number of stories in which minorities are portrayed as criminals, welfare recipients, athletes, and so on. Indeed, surveys of reporters suggest that, as a profession, journalism is arguably one of the most sympathetic to minorities and underprivileged groups (Lichter, Rothman, and Lichter 1986).

We have no quarrel with news organizations' efforts to promote diversity, but no amount of diversity or attention to minority concerns will solve the problem of racialized reporting. Ironically, it is precisely this sensitivity to diversity issues that may be undermining the quality of African Americans' news coverage. In their haste to be responsive to minority concerns, many organizations seem to be bending over backward to report on topics of interest primarily to minorities. Who better to quote in such a story than a high-ranking African American public official? In so doing, the reporter is simultaneously able to achieve two diversity goals: cover an issue that disproportionately affects minorities and portray a minority individual as good at something other than sports, entertainment, or crime.

The problem, of course, is that most news organizations operate as if quoting a minority House member in the occasional page 4 story on affirmative action or civil rights somehow eliminates any and all obligation to quote minorities in front-page stories on budget negotiations or foreign affairs. For that, a white member will almost always suffice. It is a self-imposed quota system that reduces African American members of Congress to the role of (at best) voices for the minority or (at worst) extremist fringe politicians single-mindedly pursuing their own selfish interests. Either way, a potentially harmful stereotype is perpetuated.

Our results suggest that reporters and editors will need to reevaluate their priorities for covering minorities. While reporters should continue to cover topics that affect minority communities, it is equally important that they bear in mind that minorities' interests do not all lie within a well-defined, narrow range of issues. Minority spokespeople should also be regularly cited in stories on everyday topics such as budget deficits, health care, national defense, and the environment. To shut minorities out of these stories is to imply that these are somehow "white issues," which undermines minority politicians' chances to be taken seriously as potential leaders outside minority communities. For the same reasons, reporters should make equally strong efforts to include supportive white members in stories on minority issues. In short, race should never be allowed to predetermine a political leader's relevance to any legitimate political story.

Our results also suggest that reporters should resist the temptation to identify representatives' race or the racial makeup of their districts. Except in cases where race is absolutely central to the story, there are almost no instances where a racial label seems appropriate. Consider again an excerpt from the Knight-Ridder story on John Conyers presented in Chapter 1:

When Detroit gained a majority-black district in 1964, he ran for it and won, becoming the second black person to represent the city in Congress. He became the consummate grassroots advocate, thriving on the turbulence of Vietnam and the Civil Rights era. He went to sit-ins. Fifteen years ago, Conyers successfully pushed through a bill to create a Martin Luther King holiday.[2]

By contrast, imagine the outcry if another key figure in the impeachment process were reported on with the same level of emphasis on race:

Elected to Congress in 1978, Jim Sensenbrenner is one of several successive whites to represent Wisconsin's 98% white 9th district. The Judiciary Committee's second ranking Republican has spent his entire career fighting for lower taxes and reduced government spending — issues that are very important to his white constituents. A few years ago, Sensenbrenner proved himself worthy of his constituents' support by voting against the Civil Rights Act of 1991.

Were such a report ever to make it out of the newsroom and into print, observers would surely condemn it for injecting race into a story where race played no substantive role. The default assumption would probably be that the story was trying to make a point about the power of whites in American society, and the reporter might even be labeled a racist.

Consider the reverberations of the *Washington Post's* coverage of the 1999 Baltimore mayoral election. When Martin O'Malley won the Democratic primary, the *Washington Post's* front-page headline read: "White Man Gets Mayoral Nomination in Baltimore."[3]

The headline struck many readers as both inexplicable and sad. One told the paper, "It made me cringe. It was just ghastly. It feels like it's 1968."[4] Another labeled the headline "extremely offensive" and said it "added to the racial divide."[5]

The day after the headline ran, the *Post* found itself apologizing, suggesting that it had "distorted the role of race in the election" and "violated *Washington Post* policy about reporting racial identifications only in proper context."[6]

In a column a few days later, E. R. Shipp, the *Post* ombudsperson, wrote that "the *Post* blew it . . . it was as if editors had never heard of — or never absorbed — the oft-quoted desire of the late Martin Luther King Jr. to see America transformed into a place where people 'will not be judged by the color of their skin but by the content of their character.'"[7]

That a highly respected newspaper would inject race into politics represents a pattern that is all too common. As Shipp writes, the situation clearly revealed an "ineptness in dealing with race and ethnicity."[8] But by listening to the reaction of its readers, by thinking about the fairness of its coverage, by considering what should have been done, instead of merely moving onto the next story and the next opportunity to inject race into political coverage, the *Post*'s editorial team will have the chance to learn from this experience.

Ironically, though, the very uniqueness of "racializing" coverage of a white politician brought attention to this portrayal and garnered apologies from the *Post*.

Yet, because a minority member of Congress is still viewed as a peculiar political phenomenon, many reporters see nothing wrong with reporting on African American members in precisely the same racialized fashion. Indeed, most of the reporters we surveyed would apparently not think twice about identifying the race of a minority politician under most circumstances. After all, "it's true, isn't it?"

It may be true, but reporters must come to realize that, because they are disproportionately mentioned in conjunction with minority causes, identifying the race of minority members is likely to be especially harmful. When voters are bombarded with stories of "black representatives" from "black districts" who seem interested only in "black causes," is it any wonder that minority politicians have a difficult time garnering electoral support from whites? Of course, most journalists who engage in this practice are neither racist nor intent on creating racial disharmony — in fact, quite the opposite is probably true — but this in no way lessens the very serious (if unintended) consequences of routinely identifying a spokesperson's race only when he or she is a minority. Fortunately, this problem is easily corrected, and we see no reason why congressional reporters should object to omitting racial labels in stories having nothing to do with race.

Finally, we urge members of the media to afford politicians every possible opportunity to speak for themselves. Many of the press secretaries we contacted, including those in white members' offices, complained that they were unable to get their message out to constituents without having it funneled through a journalist's interpretation. Specifically, the secretaries complained that reporters' interpretations are too often colored by unwarranted skepticism and occasionally demonstrate a lack of preparation or knowledge of the issues at hand. Naturally, the journalist's role should never be reduced to that of a mere bullhorn for potentially dishonest or demagogic politicians, but neither should a journalist stand in the way of free-flowing communication between our representatives and the represented.

Members of Congress want to be portrayed in a positive light, and most hope that journalists will help convey favorable images back to the district. But what the press secretaries seem to genuinely want most — especially in African American offices — is not a platform to spread lies or propaganda but an opportunity to explain the member's priorities and accomplishments without first being pigeonholed as being concerned with only a limited range of issues or a specific group of constituents. They want their phones to ring and their calls returned whether the topic of the day is civil rights in America or civil rights in China, crime on Main Street or crime on Wall Street, welfare spending or military spending. This seems a reasonable expectation for any member of the U.S. Congress, and it is a request that journalists ought to grant routinely without stopping first to ask whether the topic seems "appropriate." While part of the reporter's job may be to critically evaluate the merits of what our elected officials are saying, it is first and foremost the reporter's job to listen.

Officeholders

It is ultimately the media that will need to change the balance of news coverage, but minority officeholders will probably need to shoulder some of the responsibility for effecting these changes. Many press secretaries in African American members' offices complained bitterly about media treatment, but few mentioned any concrete steps taken to change it. For obvious reasons, most politicians are wary of forming hostile relations with journalists, and most are unlikely to refuse interviews on topics that appear to be within their realm of expertise. But they must also begin to recognize that not all publicity is created equal. To the extent that it conforms with prevalent stereotypes, even seemingly positive publicity may be damaging in the long run.

In other words, minority politicians must learn to say no. Although it might seem naive to expect any politician to refuse free publicity, members of Congress are often in an excellent position to influence the content of their coverage. There is, after all, something of a symbiotic relationship between politicians and the media: politicians rely on the media for publicity, but the media — especially local media — rely on politicians as easy sources of information to help fill newspaper columns and news programs. Because they represent an irreplaceable source of news, members of Congress are often able to alter the course of their own coverage by threatening to deny access to uncooperative reporters (Cook 1989).

Thus, minority representatives should begin to selectively punish reporters who needlessly identify their race or include them only within the context of stereotypical topics, while rewarding those who omit mentions of race and treat minority members as full-fledged members capable of commenting on a wide array of topics. As we have seen, many reporters, including African American reporters, seem not to view racialized reporting as a legitimate problem. One of the primary goals of this book has been to alert the journalism community to the magnitude and consequences of racialized news coverage, but it may well be minority officeholders themselves who are uniquely positioned to effect changes in journalistic standards.

Academics

There is still much to be learned about media coverage of minority politicians. The preceding study has several obvious limitations, leaving many important questions yet unanswered.

Do our findings, for example, apply to racial and ethnic minorities other than African Americans? Is there a similar bias in coverage of women members? What about coverage of members who fall into two or more minority groups, such as African American women? Does racialized reporting have a similar effect on the public's perception of minorities holding lower offices? Is there a difference between print and broadcast news coverage? Do they have different effects on public opinion?

There are, of course, many issues besides racialized news for future media studies to tackle. However, it is surely time we stop endlessly rediscovering the fact that news coverage lacks substance and focuses too heavily on crime and tragedy. Racialized media coverage poses an entirely new set of important questions, and our ability to answer these questions may ultimately determine whether America evolves into a fully integrated society or remains forever divided by race. It is hard to imagine a more worthy topic of inquiry.

The Consumer

Like most American industries, news media are driven by their bottom line. The profit motive is largely responsible for racialized media coverage, as it encourages reporters to rely on well-established routines for generating quick and easy news stories and to focus on topics that are potentially controversial and intriguing. Racialized reporting is a natural by-product of a news-for-profit mentality.

Fortunately, the profit motive also ensures that news organizations will generally comply with what they believe the public wants to read and hear. This means that average citizens can usually get better media coverage simply by making a collective demand for it, and curbing the use of racialized reporting is no exception. It is therefore important that citizens contact news providers to point out instances where race has been allowed to overshadow substantive issues or distort coverage of minority politicians. A few short letters, phone calls, or e-mails may go a long way toward reducing the prevalence of racialized reporting.

Ultimately, as the *Washington Post*'s E. R. Shipp points out, racialized coverage is "a problem" to which "attention, as they say, must be paid."[9] However we go about it, it is imperative that we begin looking for ways to overcome racialized news. In the words of the student cited at the beginning of the chapter, "change is needed to show what Blacks are truly capable of . . . thereby preventing a wrong and inferior or even hateful image of them." We could not agree more.

NOTES

1. The essay is available at http://www.fred.net/nhhs/ essays/gabbie.txt
2. *Toronto Star*, September 13, 1998.
3. *Washington Post*, September 14, 1999.
4. Ibid.
5. *Washington Post*, September 19, 1999.
6. *Washington Post*, September 15, 1999.
7. *Washington Post*, September 19, 1999.
8. Ibid.
9. Ibid.

Appendix

Reporter Survey Materials

COVER LETTER

My colleague and I are engaged in a study to better understand media coverage of Congress, and explore the often heard charge that coverage reflects a partisan bias on the part of the media.

Given the vehemence of some political candidates and many voters, we would particularly value the reporter's perception of Congressional coverage and of the Congress itself.

We would appreciate it very much if you would take a few minutes to answer the enclosed questions, and return them in the postage paid envelope. In order to pursue an accurate picture of media coverage, we would highly value your practitioners' viewpoint.

This is a completely confidential and anonymous process. We will not refer, nor will we record, any respondent's name in this project. This research project is funded by the non-partisan American Political Science Association.

We know you are very busy, and as a token of our appreciation for your time, we will be making a $5 donation to an educational scholarship fund for every survey returned.

You may receive a summary of the results of this study by writing your name and address on the back of the return envelope, or by requesting a summary under separate cover. Please do not put this information on the question sheet itself.

For your information, we have attached a summary of our first set of results in our ongoing study of partisan bias, examining charges of bias in coverage of governors.

I would be most happy to answer any questions you might have. Please feel free to write, email, call, or fax.

Thank you for your assistance.

Sincerely,

David Niven, Ph.D.
Florida Atlantic University

Jeremy Zilber, Ph.D.
College of William and Mary

Summary of "Partisan Bias in the Media? A New Test" by David Niven, to be published in *Social Science Quarterly*, 1999

Allegations of partisan bias in the media are familiar refrains emanating both from Republican candidates and from a number of recent scholarly studies. This research tests for the existence of bias in a significantly more objective fashion than has been employed in previous work. Utilizing a database of 20 years of newspaper coverage of governors, this study compares media reaction to governors of opposing parties who have produced comparable results with regard to their states' murder and unemployment rates. Thus, differences in media coverage that emerge can logically be attributed to bias. The data, however, offer no support to allegations of bias, as the treatment of Democrats and Republicans in similar situations is nearly indistinguishable. In addition to deflating the argument that the media are biased against Republicans, this study provides a model test for studying media bias that can be applied to various political actors and political issues. This test can also be utilized to gauge other media tendencies, such as their propensity to be negative.

SURVEY ON MEDIA AND CONGRESS

Please keep in mind that there are no right or wrong answers to these questions, we are simply seeking your expert opinion.

Feel free to make any extra comments you have in the margins.

1. On a scale of A to F (A=excellent, F=failing), how would you rate the job done by Members of Congress in fulfilling their duties and obligations?

>   A
>   B
>   C
>   D
>   F

Would you agree or disagree with the following assertions about Members of Congress:

2. Members of Congress too often do not think for themselves.

>   AGREE
>   DISAGREE

3. Members generally know or understand only a few issues.

>   AGREE
>   DISAGREE

4. Members would rather get their names in the paper than get a bill passed.

>   AGREE
>   DISAGREE

5. It is hard to get an honest answer from a Member of Congress.

>   AGREE
>   DISAGREE

6. Congress would be better, and the American people would be better off, if there were more former reporters serving in Congress.

>   AGREE
>   DISAGREE

7. In your personal opinion, do these members of Congress have the following traits. Please check as many boxes as you think apply to each person.

	Hard-working	Trust-worthy	Has Best Interests of Country in Mind	Too Partisan	Open Minded	Credit to Their Profession
Richard Gephardt						
Tom Delay						
John Conyers						
Barbara Boxer						
Kay Bailey Hutchinson						
Charles Rangel						
Tom Daschle						
J.C. Watts						
Dick Armey						
David Bonior						
Maxine Waters						
Trent Lott						

8. On a scale of A to F (A=excellent, F=failing), how would you rate the job
    done by members of the media in reporting on the Congress?

    > A
    > B
    > C
    > D
    > F

Comments_____

_____

9. Which of these best describes your opinion of media coverage of Congress?

    FAIR TO BOTH DEMOCRATS AND REPUBLICANS
    BIASED AGAINST DEMOCRATS
    BIASED AGAINST REPUBLICANS

10. In your personal opinion, do these members of the media have the following traits. Please check as many boxes as you think apply to each person.

	Hard-working	Trustworthy	Has Best Interests of Country in Mind	Too Partisan	Open Minded	Credit to Their Profession
Jack Germond, *The Sun*						
Bernie Shaw, CNN						
Maureen Dowd, *New York Times*						
Bob Woodward, *Washington Post*						
Clarence Page, *Chicago Tribune*						
George Will, ABC/ columnist						
David Broder, *Washington Post*						
Molly Ivins, *Fort Worth Star-Telegram*						
Bob Herbert, *New York Times*						
Dan Rather, CBS						
Dewayne Wickham, *USA TODAY*						
Sam Donaldson, ABC						

For the purposes of ensuring a well rounded sample, would you please share some basic information about yourself.

11. Your race

> WHITE
> BLACK/AFRICAN AMERICAN
> HISPANIC/LATINO
> ASIAN AMERICAN
> OTHER_____

12. Your gender

> MALE
> FEMALE

13. How many years have you worked as a reporter?

> _____

Thank you very much for your participation.

You may receive a summary of the results of this study by writing your name and address on the back of the return envelope, or by requesting a summary under separate cover. Please do not put this information on the question sheet itself.

Bibliography

Barber, John, and Oscar Gandy. 1990. "Press Portrayal of African American and White United States Representatives." *Howard Journal of Communications* 2: 213-225.

Barone, Michael, and Grant Ujifusa. 1997. *The Almanac of American Politics, 1998.* Washington, D.C.: National Journal.

Bell, L. S. 1973. "The Role and Performance of Black and Metro Newspapers in Relation to Political Campaigns in Selected Racially Mixed Congressional Elections." Ph.D. dissertation, Northwestern University.

Bennett, W. Lance. 1988. *News: The Politics of Illusion.* New York: Longman.

Bennett, W. Lance. 1990. "Toward a Theory of Press-State Relations in the United States." *Journal of Communication* 40: 103-125.

Beyle, Thad, Donald Ostdiek, and G. Patrick Lynch. 1996. "Is the State Press Corp Biased?" *Spectrum: The Journal of State Government* 69: 6-16.

Bobo, Lawrence, and Franklin Gilliam. 1993. "Race, Sociopolitical Participation, and Empowerment." *American Political Science Review* 84: 377-393.

Broh, C. Anthony. 1987. *A Horse of a Different Color: Television's Treatment of Jesse Jackson's 1984 Presidential Campaign.* Washington, DC: Joint Center for Political Studies.

Brown, J., R. Collins, and G. Schmidt. 1988. "Self-Esteem and Direct Versus Indirect Forms of Self-Enhancement." *Journal of Personality and Social Psychology* 55: 445-453.

Burnstein, E., and A. Vinokur. 1975. "What a Person Thinks upon Learning He Has Chosen Differently from Others." *Journal of Experimental Social Psychology* 11: 412-426.

Byrd, Joann. 1997. "Blacks, Whites in News Pictures." In *Facing Difference: Race, Gender, and Mass Media*, Shirley Biagi and Marylin Kern-Foxworth (eds.). Thousand Oaks, CA: Pine Forge Press.

Cameron, Charles, David Epstein, and Sharyn O'Halloran. 1996. "Do Majority-Minority Districts Maximize Substantive Black Representation in Congress?" *American Political Science Review* 90: 794-812.

Campbell, Christopher. 1995. *Race, Myth and the News*. Thousand Oaks, CA: Sage.

Carpenter, S. 1993. "Organization of In-Group and Out-Group Information: The Influence of Gender-Role Information." *Social Cognition* 11: 70-91.

Cavanaugh, Thomas. 1983. *Race and Political Strategy*. Baltimore: Johns Hopkins University Press.

Chaudhary, Anju. 1980. "Press Portrayal of Black Officials." *Journalism Quarterly* 57: 636-646.

Clawson, Rosalee A. and Ryan Tom. 1999. "Media Coverage of State Legislators: Is There a Gender Bias?" Presented at the Annual Meeting of the Midwest Political Science Association.

Citrin, Jack, Donald Green, and David Sears. 1990. "White Reactions to Black Candidates." *Public Opinion Quarterly* 54: 74-96.

Clarke, Peter, and Susan Evans. 1983. *Covering Campaigns: Journalism in Congressional Elections*. Stanford, CA: Stanford University Press.

Clay, William. 1992. *Just Permanent Interests: Black Americans in Congress, 1870-1991*. New York: Amistad Press.

Cook, Timothy. 1986. "House Members as Newsmakers: The Effects of Televising Congress." *Legislative Studies Quarterly* 11: 203-226.

Cook, Timothy. 1989. *Making Laws and Making News*. Washington, DC: Brookings.

Croteau, David, and William Hoynes. 1994. *By Invitation Only: How the Media Limit Political Debate*. Monroe, ME: Common Courage.

Dates, Jannette, and William Barlow. 1993. *Split Image: African Americans in the Mass Media*. Washington, DC: Howard University Press.

Davis, Jessica, and Oscar Gandy. 1999. "Racial Identity and Media Orientation: Exploring the Nature of Constraint." *Journal of Black Studies* 29: 367-397.

Devine, P. 1989. "Stereotypes and Prejudice: Their Automatic and Controlled Components." *Journal of Personality and Social Psychology* 56: 5-18.

Dewhirst, Robert. 1983. "Patterns of Interaction between Members of the U.S. House of Representatives and Their Home District News Media." Ph.D. dissertation, University of Nebraska.

Dickson, Sandra. 1994. "Understanding Media Bias: The Press and the U.S. Invasion of Panama." *Journalism Quarterly* 71: 809-819.

Duncan, Philip, and Christine Lawrence. 1997. *Politics in America, 1998*. Washington, DC: Congressional Quarterly Press.

Eagly, A., M. Makhijani, and B. Klonsky. 1992. "Gender and the Evaluation of Leaders: A Meta-Analysis." *Psychological Bulletin* 111: 3-32.

Eagly, A., and A. Mladinic. 1989. "Gender Stereotypes and Attitudes toward Women and Men." *Personality and Social Psychology Bulletin* 15: 543-558.

Eagly, A., and W. Wood. 1982. "Inferred Sex Differences in Status as a Determinant of Gender Stereotypes about Social Influence." *Journal of Personality and Social Psychology* 43: 915-928.

Entman, Robert. 1989. "How the Media Affect What People Think: An Information Processing Approach." *Journal of Politics* 51: 347-370.

Entman, Robert. 1992. "Blacks in the News: Television, Modern Racism and Cultural Change." *Journalism Quarterly* 69: 341-361.

Entman, Robert. 1994. "Representation and Reality in the Portrayal of Blacks on Network Television News." *Journalism Quarterly* 71: 509-520.

Entman, Robert. 1997. "African Americans according to TV News." In *The Media in Black and White*, Everette E. Dennis and Edward C. Pease (eds.). New Brunswick, NJ: Transaction.

Fallows, James. 1997. *Breaking the News: How the Media Undermine American Democracy*. New York: Vintage Books.

Fenno, Richard. 1978. *Home Style: House Members in Their Districts*. Boston: Little, Brown.

Fiske, Susan, and Shelley Taylor. 1991. *Social Cognition*. New York: McGraw-Hill.

Frady, Marshall. 1968. *Wallace*. Cleveland: NAL.

Galtung, J., and M. H. Ruge. 1970. "The Structure of Foreign News." In *Media Sociology*, Jeremey Tunstall (ed.). Urbana: University of Illinois Press.

Gans, Herbert. 1980. *Deciding What's News*. New York: Vintage.

Gerber, Alan. 1996. "African Americans' Congressional Careers and the Democratic House Delegation." *Journal of Politics* 58: 831-845.

Gibbons, Arnold. 1993. *Race, Politics, and the White Media: The Jesse Jackson Campaigns*. Lanham, MD: University Press of America.

Gilens, Martin. 1995. "Race and Poverty in America: Public Misperceptions and the American News Media." Presented at the Annual Meeting of the American Political Science Association.

Giles, Michael, and Arthur Evans. 1987. "External Threat, Perceived Threat, and Group Identity." *Social Science Quarterly* 68: 50-65.

Glynn, Carroll J., Susan Herbst, Garrett J. O'Keefe, and Robert Y. Shapiro. 1999. *Public Opinion*. Boulder, CO: Westview.

Goidel, Robert, and Todd Shields. 1994. "The Vanishing Marginals, the Bandwagon, and the Mass Media." *Journal of Politics* 56: 802-810.

Gow, David John, and Robert Eubank. 1984. "The Pro-Incumbent Bias in the 1982 National Election Study." *American Journal of Political Science* 28: 224-230.

Graber, Doris A. 1997. *Mass Media and American Politics*. Washington, DC: Congressional Quarterly Press.

Grainey, Timothy, Dennis Pollack, and Lori Kusmierek. 1984. "How Three Chicago Newspapers Covered the Washington-Epton Campaign." *Journalism Quarterly* 61: 352-363.

Groeling, Tim, and Samuel Kernell. 1998. "Is Network News Coverage of the President Biased?" *Journal of Politics* 60: 1063-1087.

Gunther, Albert. 1992. "Biased Press or Biased Public?" *Public Opinion Quarterly* 56: 147-167.

Hamilton, D. L., and R. K. Gifford. 1976. "Illusory Correlation in Interpersonal Perception: A Cognitive Basis of Stereotypic Judgments." *Journal of Experimental Social Psychology* 12: 392-407.

Hess, Stephen. 1994. "The Decline and Fall of Congressional News." In *Congress, the Press, and the Public,* Thomas Mann and Norman Ornstein (eds.). Washington, DC: American Enterprise Institute.

Hoffman, C., and N. Hurst. 1990. "Gender Stereotypes: Perception or Rationalization." *Journal of Personality and Social Psychology* 58: 197-208.

Hofstetter, C. Richard. 1976. *Bias in the News: Network Television Coverage of the 1972 Campaign.* Columbus: Ohio State University Press.

Huckfeldt, Robert, and Carol Kohfeld. 1989. *Race and the Decline of Class in American Politics.* Urbana: University of Illinois Press.

Jackman, M., and M. Muha. 1984. "Education and Intergroup Attitudes." *American Sociological Review* 49: 751-769.

Jamieson, D. W., and M. Zanna. 1989. "Need for Structure in Attitude Formation and Expression." In *Attitude Structure and Function,* A. R. Pratkinis, S. J. Breckler, and A. G. Greenwood (eds.). Hillsdale, NJ: Lawrence Erlbaum Associates.

Jennings, M. Kent, and Richard G. Niemi. 1981. *Generations and Politics: A Panel Study of Young Adults and Their Parents.* Princeton, NJ: Princeton University Press.

Jones, Charles, and Michael Clemons. 1993. "A Model of Racial Crossover Voting: An Assessment of the Wilder Victory." In *Dilemmas of Black Politics,* Georgia Persons (ed.). New York: HarperCollins.

Jones, E., G. Wood, and G. Quattrone. 1981. "Perceived Variability of Personal Characteristics in In-Groups and Out-Groups." *Personality and Social Psychology Bulletin* 7: 523-528.

Judd, C., and B. Park. 1988. "Out-Group Homogeneity: Judgements of Variability at the Individual and Group Levels." *Journal of Personality and Social Psychology* 54: 778-788.

Jussim, L. 1990. "Social Reality and Social Problems: The Role of Expectancies." *Journal of Social Issues* 46: 9-34.

Just, Marion. 1997. "Candidate Strategies and the Media Campaign." In *The Election of 1996,* Gerald Pomper (ed.). Chatham, NJ: Chatham House.

Kahan, Michael. 1999. *Media as Politics: Theory, Behavior, and Change in America.* Upper Saddle River, NJ: Prentice-Hall.

Kahn, Kim Fridkin. 1996. *The Political Consequences of Being a Woman*. New York: Columbia University Press.

Keever, Beverly A. D. 1997. "The Origins and Colors of a News Gap." In *U.S. News Coverage of Racial Minorities*, Beverly A.D. Keever, Carolyn Martindale, and Mary Ann Weston (eds.). Westport, CT: Greenwood Press.

Kenney, Patrick, and Tom Rice. 1984. "The Effect of Primary Divisiveness in Gubernatorial and Senatorial Elections." *Journal of Politics* 46: 904-915.

Kiesler, S. B. 1975. "Actuarial Prejudice toward Women and Its Implications." *Journal of Applied Social Psychology* 5: 201-216.

Kinder, Donald R., and Lynn M. Sanders. 1996. *Divided by Color: Racial Politics and Democratic Ideals*. Chicago: University of Chicago Press.

Klahr, D. 1969. "Decision Making in a Complex Environment: The Use of Similarity Judgements to Predict Preferences." *Management Science* 15: 593-618.

Kleppner, Paul. 1985. *Chicago Divided: The Making of a Black Mayor*. Dekalb: Northern Illinois University Press.

Koller, M., and R. Wicklund. 1988. "Press and Task Difficulty as Determinants of Preoccupation with Person Descriptors." *Journal of Experimental Social Psychology* 24: 256-274.

Kruglanski, A. W. 1989. *Lay Epistemics and Human Knowledge*. New York: Plenum.

Kurtz, Howard. 1994. *Media Circus*. New York: Random House.

Lau, R., and D. Russell. 1980. "Attributions in the Sports Pages." *Journal of Personality and Social Psychology* 39: 29-38.

Lester, Paul, and Ron Smith. 1990. "African-American Photo Coverage in *Life, Newsweek, and Time*, 1937-1988." *Journalism Quarterly* 67: 128-136.

Levine, Lawrence. 1977. *Black Culture and Black Consciousness*. New York: Oxford University Press.

Lichter, S. Robert, Stanley Rothman, and Linda Lichter. 1986. *The Media Elite*. Bethesda, MD: Adler and Adler.

Mackie, D., and L. Worth. 1989. "Differential Recall of Subcategory Information about In-Group and Out-Group Members." *Personality and Social Psychology Bulletin* 15: 401-413.

MacKuen, Michael. 1984. "Exposure to Information, Belief Integration, and Individual Responsiveness to Agenda Change." *American Political Science Review* 78: 372-391.

Maisel, Sandy. 1982. *From Obscurity to Oblivion: Running in the Congressional Primary*. Knoxville: University of Tennessee Press.

Markus, Gregory, and Philip Converse. 1979. "A Dynamic Simultaneous Equation Model of Electoral Choice." *American Political Science Review* 73: 1055-1070.

Martindale, Carolyn. 1986. *The White Press and Black America*. Westport, CT: Greenwood Press.

Martindale, Carolyn, and Lillian Rae Dunlap. 1997. "The African Americans." In *U.S. News Coverage of Racial Minorities*, Beverly A. D. Keever, Carolyn Martindale, and Mary Ann Weston (eds.). Westport, CT: Greenwood Press.

McCombs, Maxwell, and Donald Shaw. 1977. *The Emergence of American Political Issues*. St. Paul, MN: West.

McCormack, Joseph, and Charles Jones. 1993. "The Conceptualization of Deracialization: Thinking Through the Dilemma." In *Dilemmas of Black Politics*, Georgia Persons (ed.). New York: HarperCollins.

McGuire, William. 1985. "Attitudes and Attitude Change." In *The Handbook of Social Psychology*, E. Aronson and G. Lindzey (eds.). New York: Random House.

Miller, Susan. 1976. "Congress and the News Media: Coverage, Collaboration and Agenda-Setting." Ph.D. dissertation, Stanford University.

Miller, Susan. 1977. "News Coverage of Congress: The Search for the Ultimate Spokesman." *Journalism Quarterly* 54: 459-465.

Mondak, Jeffrey. 1995. "Competence, Integrity, and the Electoral Success of Congressional Incumbents." *Journal of Politics* 57: 1043-1069.

Neuman, W. Russell. 1986. *The Paradox of Mass Politics, Knowledge and Opinion in the American Electorate*. Cambridge: Harvard University Press.

New York Times Manual of Style and Usage. 1976. New York: Times Books.

Niven, David. 1998. *The Missing Majority: The Recruitment of Women as State Legislative Candidates*. Westport, CT: Praeger.

Niven, David. 1999. "Partisan Bias in the Media? A New Test." *Social Science Quarterly* 80: 847-858.

Niven, David, and Jeremy Zilber. 1996. "Media Treatment of Minorities in Congress: Coverage and Its Effects." Presented at the Annual Meeting of the Southern Political Science Association.

Niven, David, and Jeremy Zilber. 1998. "What's Newt Doing in *People* Magazine? The Changing Effect of National Prominence in Congressional Elections." *Political Behavior* 20: 213-224.

Page, Benjamin, and Calvin Jones. 1979. "Reciprocal Effects of Policy Preferences, Party Loyalties, and the Vote." *American Political Science Review* 73: 1071-1089.

Paletz, David, and Robert Entman. 1981. *Media Power Politics*. New York: Free Press.

Parker, Glenn. 1981. "Interpreting Candidate Awareness in U.S. Congressional Elections." *Legislative Studies Quarterly* 6: 219-234.

Parker, Kimberly Coursen. 1994. "How the Press Views Congress." In *Congress, the Press, and the Public,* Thomas Mann and Norman Ornstein (eds.). Washington, DC: American Enterprise Institute.

Patterson, Thomas. 1994. *Out of Order*. New York: Vintage.

Patterson, Thomas, and Robert McClure. 1976. *The Unseeing Eye*. New York: Putnam.

Payne, J. Gregory. 1988. "Shaping the Race Issue: A Special Kind of Journalism." *Political Communication and Persuasion* 5: 145-160.

Payne, James. 1980. "Show Horses and Work Horses in the United States House of Representatives." *Polity* 12: 428-456.

Pettigrew, Thomas, and Denise Alston. 1988. *Tom Bradley's Campaigns for Governor*. Washington, DC: Joint Center for Political Studies.

Piliavin, J. 1987. "Age, Race, and Sex Similarity to Candidates and Voting Preference." *Journal of Applied Social Psychology* 17: 351-368.

Rainville, R., and E. McCormick. 1977. "Extent of Covert Racial Prejudice in Pro Football Announcers' Speech." *Journalism Quarterly* 54: 20-26.

Reeves, Keith. 1997. *Voting Hopes or Fears? White Voters, Black Candidates and Racial Politics in America*. New York: Oxford University Press.

Riffe, Daniel, Don Sneed, and Roger Van Ommeren. 1989. "The Press and Black Elected Officials at Three Levels of Public Office." Presented at the Annual Meeting of the Association for Education in Journalism and Mass Communication.

Robinson, Michael, and Margaret Sheehan. 1983. *Over the Wire and on TV*. New York: Russell Sage Foundation.

Romer, Daniel, Kathleen Jamieson, and Nicole Coteau. 1998. "The Treatment of Persons of Color in Local Television News." *Communication Research* 25: 286-305.

Sears, David, Jack Citrin, and Rick Kosterman. 1987. "Jesse Jackson and the Southern White Electorate in 1984." In *Blacks in Southern Politics*, Lawrence Moreland, Robert Steed, and Tod Baker (eds.). New York: Praeger.

Sentman, Mary Alice. 1983. "Black and White: Disparity in Coverage by Life Magazine from 1937 to 1972." *Journalism Quarterly* 60: 501-508.

Shaw, Daron, and Bartholomew Sparrow. 1999. "From the Inner Ring Out: News Congruence, Cue-Taking, and Campaign Coverage." *Political Research Quarterly* 52: 323-351.

Sigelman, Lee, and Steven A. Tuch. 1997. "Metastereotypes: Blacks' Perceptions of Whites' Stereotypes of Blacks." *Public Opinion Quarterly* 61: 87-101

Sigelman, Lee, and Susan Welch. 1991. *Black Americans' Views of Racial Inequality: The Dream Deferred*. Cambridge, MA: Cambridge University Press.

Smith, Tom W. 1992. "Changing Racial Labels from 'Colored' to 'Negro' to 'Black' to 'African American.'" *Public Opinion Quarterly* 56: 496-514.

Sneed, Don, Daniel Riffe, and Roger Van Ommeren. 1988. "Press Coverage of Blacks and the Black Community: The Minority Legislator's Perspective." Presented at the Annual Meeting of the Association for Education in Journalism and Mass Communication.

Sniderman, Paul, Carol Swain, and Laurel Elms. 1995. "The Dynamics of a Senate Campaign: Incumbency, Ideology, and Race." Presented at the Annual Meeting of the American Political Science Association.

Snyder, M. 1984. "When Belief Creates Reality." In *Advances in Experimental Social Psychology*, L. Berkowitz (ed.). San Diego: Academic Press.

Stempel, G. 1971. "Visibility of Blacks in the News and News-Picture Magazines." *Journalism Quarterly* 48: 337-339.

Swain, Carol. 1995. *Black Faces, Black Interests: The Representation of African Americans in Congress*. Cambridge: Harvard University Press.

Terkildsen, Nayda. 1996. "Media Coverage of Congressional Elections: Linking African American Candidates to Their Race." Presented at the Annual Meeting of the Midwest Political Science Association.

Tidmarch, Charles, and John Pitney. 1985. "Covering Congress." *Polity* 17: 446-483.

Turner, J., R. Brown, and H. Tajfel. 1979. "Social Comparison and Group Interest in Ingroup Favoritism." *European Journal of Social Psychology* 9: 187-204.

Vallone, Robert, Lee Ross, and Mark Lepper. 1985. "The Hostile Media Phenomenon: Biased Perception and Perceptions of Media Bias in Coverage of the Beirut Massacre." *Journal of Personality and Social Psychology* 49: 577-585.

Van Dijk, Teun. 1991. *Racism and the Press*. Routledge.

Watts, Mark, David Domke, Dhavan Shah, and David Fan. 1999. "Elite Cues and Media Bias in Presidential Campaigns." *Communication Research* 26: 144-175.

Weaver, David H., and G. Cleveland Wilhoit. 1996. *The American Journalist in the 1990s*. Mahwah, NJ: Lawrence Erlbaum Associates.

Wilson, Clint, and Felix Gutierrez. 1985. *Minorities and the Media*. Beverly Hills, CA: Sage.

Witt, Linda, Karen Paget, and Glenna Matthews. 1995. *Running as a Woman*. New York: Free Press.

Yount, K. 1986. "A Theory of Productive Activity: The Relationships Among Self-Concept, Gender, Sex Role Stereotypes, and Work-Emergent Traits." *Psychology of Women Quarterly* 10: 63-88.

Zaller, John, and Dennis Chiu. 1996. "Government's Little Helper: U.S. Press Coverage of Foreign Policy Crises, 1945-1991." *Political Communication* 13: 385-405.

Zilber, Jeremy, and David Niven. 1995. "'Black' versus 'African American': Are Whites' Political Attitudes Influenced by the Choice of Racial Labels?" *Social Science Quarterly* 76: 655-664.

Index

About the Authors

JEREMY ZILBER teaches American politics, media, public opinion, and campaigns courses at the College of William and Mary.

DAVID NIVEN teaches American politics, media, campaigns, and women and politics courses at Florida Atlantic University. He is the author of *The Missing Majority: The Recruitment of Women as State Legislative Candidates* (Praeger, 1998).

ISBN 0-275-96841-3

90000>

EAN

9 780275 968410

HARDCOVER BAR CODE